STEPPING
STONES

STEPPING STONES

A *Memoir of* Addiction, Loss, *and* Transformation

MARILEA C. RABASA

She Writes Press, a BookSparks imprint
A Division of SparkPointStudio, LLC.

Published 2020

Printed in the United States of America

ISBN: 978-1-63152-898-9
ISBN: 978-1-63152-899-6
Library of Congress Control Number: 2020901459

For information, address:
She Writes Press
1569 Solano Ave #546
Berkeley, CA 94707

She Writes Press is a division of SparkPoint Studio, LLC.

AUTHOR'S NOTE

To write this work of nonfiction, I have relied on my memory of the many places I have lived and all the accompanying details and perceptions that are uniquely mine. I have done my best to be honest, true, and faithful to the retelling of my life as it has unfolded. The names of many individuals in this book have been changed in order to protect their privacy. Other family members were consulted to preserve authenticity and add clarity.

I've altered the names of some places and other distinguishing features. My personal journals as well as my mother's diaries and travel journals have added some valuable perspectives to much of my life story.

A letter to my grandchildren

Dear Cate and Ems,

Open the door to your imagination as you observe the world around you!
Did you see the Olympic Mountains today from your living room window?
In the morning as the sun rises in the east, slowly shining on those mountains to the west,
They might look like ice cream cones with chocolate sauce dripping down.

Pay close attention to what's happening in your world.
If good things are happening, embrace them and be grateful.
If bad things are happening, try to make them better.
Believe in all the possibilities of all the tomorrows, that better days
will come.

Never lose your capacity for wonder, and when you feel inspired, write
down your thoughts.
They light the pathway to who you once were, who you are now, who you
will be.
Like breadcrumbs in the dark, they offer clues to the "Whys?" of things.

Celebrate yourselves and the world around you!
That, my dear ones, is what matters the most to me.
For I love you to the moon and back.

—*Bela*

There is a cry deeper than all sound
whose serrated edges cut the heart
as we break open to the place inside
which is unbreakable and whole,
while learning to sing.

From "The Unbroken" by Rashani Réa[1]

CONTENTS

Part Two: MUDDLING THROUGH THE MIDDLE

Part Three: WAKING UP

Preface:
GOING HOME

September 2009

"Marilea, don't go home yet. I've barely seen you." Mother wore a wide smile, trying to conceal her neediness, as she gripped my hand.

Mama, let go . . . let go . . . let go . . .

Refusing to release my hand, she pressed on, "Do you really believe it, that there's life after death?"

"Oh, Mother, of course there is!" I lectured, straightening my spine. "What would Grammy think if she knew all those years of going to church had come to this?" I laughed, trying to make light of her fears.

Catching myself, I softened my tone. *Growing old and knowing that each day could be your last must be the loneliest place in the world.* I felt sympathetic toward the woman who had done her best for her family. *Pay attention and take notes, Marilea. You'll be on that bed someday,* I thought, glancing at my reflection in her mirror.

Laughing with me now—she had the most dazzling smile— she relaxed her grip on my hand as I turned to leave the nursing home.

I was tired and had no desire in that naked moment to continue talking about life after death. My mother, more than anything, was afraid. Just as I had learned in recent years to let go of the things I couldn't control, I wished for her that she would be able to let go of her grip on life and die peacefully.

"Sorry, I've got to run now," I said as I scanned the room for my purse, "but I'll come to say goodbye before going back to Virginia. Eat your dinner tonight. It's sole, your favorite," I instructed, warmly embracing her on the bed. As I hurried into the hall, anxious to get behind the wheel of my car, I called out over my shoulder, "I love you!"

"Bye, baby. I love you too!"

I didn't dare to linger, didn't dare to crush her frail body with all the forgiveness and love a daughter could feel. I had done my best to make peace with her years before, and we simply enjoyed each other at this point in our lives. But how I wished I could make her passing easier.

Perhaps I already had; perhaps our discussions helped her harness her faith, the faith she had found at St. Ann's on Long Island nearly a century before.

Mother was ninety-nine years old with terminal lung cancer, a particularly harsh sentence for a person who had only smoked an occasional cigarette. As the mass continued to grow in her lung, she often struggled to breathe. Hospice had recently been brought in, and the staff was authorized to put some crushed morphine under her tongue when she panicked and called for assistance. It worked well to calm and relax her. Usually she fell asleep.

Would this be the last ten-hour car trip up to Massachusetts I'd make to see her? This was the ever-present question in my mind. Every year since 1991 when I'd returned from overseas with my children, I made annual summer visits to see her and the rest of my family. After retiring, a year before she died, I was able to visit her much more frequently, and I'm grateful for that.

At the nursing home the next day, my mother was sitting up in her chair waiting for me with another Rosamunde Pilcher book on her lap.

"You really enjoy this author, don't you?" I kissed her, taking the book out of her lap to look at.

"Oh yes, I love reading about families," she said, as if there were a great distance between us. "Do you still have my copy of *The Shell Seekers?*"

"Yes. Do you want it back? I loved the movie with Angela Lansbury, though the ending was different from the book."

"Yes, I saw it too. But movies usually have happy endings." She seemed distracted.

I know what you're thinking about, but I need to change the subject. We'd hashed to death the subject of our family many times over the years, and there seemed no point in revisiting the topic just then. *I've accepted the way things were, and for the most part so have you, Mama. There are some things you just have to let go.* I hoped she could be grateful for the many blessings in her long life—that she would be able to pass on peacefully with a full heart.

Perhaps the emotion of the moment brought it on, but she started struggling for air, and I went to get the nurse. It was time for some crushed morphine.

I held her hand as she started to relax. Certain that she was asleep, I took my leave for the day. That facility was top-of-the-line, and I was so glad my sister had done all the legwork to secure a place for our mother there. Lucy was determined to see that Mother lived comfortably, and I so appreciate all she did for her. If it was the end of the road for her, then she was in a lovely place.

The next day she was noticeably incoherent, having had two morphine doses by late afternoon. I just sat on her bed for an hour and held her hand as she dozed.

I raised the pillows under her feet to improve her circulation. Then I nestled her hands just below the covers so they wouldn't feel the chill of the air-conditioning. Finally, I organized the contents of her drawers and rearranged the flowers my sister brought almost daily. None of those simple acts of tidying could prevent the very untidy act that God had in store for her.

"Bye, Ma," I said as I kissed her forehead. "I'll see you again soon. I love you."

"Bye, baby," she answered, opening her eyes, "I love you too."

In the nearly twenty years of driving from Virginia to Massachusetts to see my family, that trip was the last where I could look forward to seeing my mother.

Are we ever ready for that phone call, the one from my brother's wife that Mom had died, the one that changed me from a fatherless child into an orphan? The one telling me she had died peacefully in her sleep, just three weeks after I'd seen her? It's one of many life passages, a sobering one, assuring me that I am in fact mortal and it was now time for my siblings and me to go to the head of the line.

We have two lives . . . the life we learn with
and the life we live with after that.

—Bernard Malamud[2]

I'm living that second life—the one with learned lessons that become stepping stones to follow into the dark where learning happens. For many of us, it never ends: the wish to keep growing in our understanding of the world. I would take that one step further, on a more personal level: my need to transcend myself, to rise above my limitations to be my best in the world.

And in this world, I've traveled and lived in many countries, far from New England where I began my life. I'd hoped to find my true self in this country or that culture—as though where I lived could reconcile the tumultuous landscape inside of me. We are a sum of our parts, I've learned, yet recognizing those puzzle pieces and putting them together has been a challenge. Chameleonlike, I adapted to my surroundings. But like the lizard, I was usually afraid.

Having lived in more than twenty-five houses, I was never completely at home in any of them. Often disconnected from the communities I lived in, and even more disconnected from myself, I'd used substances in excess since childhood. Living like a gypsy kept me airborne, unable to dig down and plant roots. It became a handy excuse to avoid the mirrors that many communities provide.

What is the meaning of "home" to any of us?

For me, it would be where I'm never lonely, a place where I've arrived—where the yearning to be somewhere else vanishes. Home is where the many disparate pieces of me come together and make a whole, a place where I'm happy to stay put—and make room. I've been looking for that peaceful place my whole life.

In recent years, I've been in recovery from substance use disorder—on an inward journey—learning to accept my life and appreciate all that I have amid the disappointments. How can I, beset by sadness and instability for much of my life, come to revisit it now from another perspective? How can I learn to live beyond my ego? What has enabled me to laugh and see the comedy in things, to finally live well and be happy?

Sorrows have molded me; it's true. Substance use disorder has shaped me. Tragedies in life will inevitably leave their mark on all of us. But those of us who enjoy recovery—whether it's from alcoholism, cancer, or financial ruin—have paid some serious dues to the universe. The greater the loss, the greater the capacity for joy, as the poet William Blake reminds us, for they are irretrievably woven together.

Joyfulness is a song of the angels. Let me tell you how I've learned to sing.

Part One

SLEEPWALKING

Oh, the Places You'll Go!

—Dr. Seuss[3]

PHOTOGRAPHS

My desk looks out over Saratoga Passage, a narrow body of water between Camano Island and Whidbey Island, two of the many landmasses dotting Puget Sound in the Pacific Northwest.

A table lamp stands between two framed eight-by-ten photographs: on the left side, a color portrait of my three children taken at JCPenney's one Christmas in Miami in 1984; on the right side, a black-and-white 1951 photograph of my aunt Dodie and uncle Geo's triumphant walk down the wedding aisle. She was my father's middle sister, and she had the most stunning smile. In the foreground of the picture, there I was at the end of a pew, three years old, wearing tiny white gloves, my eyes as big as saucers, wondering how I was going to get out of there.

After the ceremony, I anxiously looked around for my brother. Bill was my one comfort—Bill and all our cats and dogs. They tell me he doted on me. Family photos in my albums confirm this. In one, I'm a toddler in a bathing suit next to my brother at a beach on Long Island. We're all smiles as we strain to see the camera, the hot summer sun in our faces. What fun we were having building castles in the sand! Ten years older than me, he would go away to boarding school before I was five.

More black-and-white snapshots call out to me, one with *1950* written at the top. It shows me at two years old on Christmas morning nestled in Bill's lap, cooing over my new doll. Our sister, Lucy, sits next to him, also holding a doll, looking at us.

Another black-and-white picture speaks to me. It's a lovely portrait of my family before I came along—Mother and Daddy, Bill at eight, and Lucy at three. Mother is a stunning woman, smiling next to Daddy, himself a handsome charmer. My sister sports lots of bouncy waves on her head to match her happy mood in that picture.

When I was born two years later, there were no more formal family portraits.

There were fulfilling family occasions recorded on film, and I'm glad to have them in a faded, grainy archive: weddings, holidays, graduations, and other milestones.

But the photographs are revealing. In my family, people didn't talk about feelings; that's just the way we were. These picture albums help me recall events and my feelings attached to them.

WALLS

"Mary, go outside and play. I need to lie down for a while," Mother pleaded, on the verge of tears. *Click* went the door latch as I approached her bedroom, the red light telling me to stop, turn around, and look elsewhere for attention. Bill was gone except for summers and holidays. Lucy was out with her friends or at ballet practice. Daddy, as usual, was in the basement. I was eight years old and lonely.

Much of the time that house felt like a vacuum after an implosion, with people pretending that everything was fine. On holidays, grown-ups walked around with drinks in their hands. I remember a big, strange-looking bottle with red lines near the kitchen sink. But the rest of the year, though I didn't see it sitting there, I didn't think things were fine.

Shut out again from being with my mother, I stopped off in the kitchen for some of her delicious apple pie and a glass of milk on my way to Daddy's basement.

SPIDERS

"**D**addy, can I come down and help you?" I called to him in the basement, my plaintive tone echoing off the basement's damp walls.

Sure, come on down. You can help me glue these parts together, I imagined he'd say. I floated down the steps until his harsh tone startled me.

Halfway down the stairs, my heart sank.

"Not now. Go check on your mother." He sounded tense and angry, in no mood for an intrusion. That's what I felt like in his and in my whole family's life—an intrusion.

"She's in bed. Told me to go outside," I responded, the wind knocked out of me by a man who preferred to be doing something else.

"Do what your mother told you," he barked, uninterested in haggling with me.

What was he doing down there all the time? Why wasn't I welcome to join him? I could smell the mustiness on the old cement walls. Some of the boulders that protruded were moss covered, with spiders lurking in dark corners.

I longed to be closer to my father, often stationing myself on the stairs leading into the cellar, hoping to catch him on the way up. Perched, little bird that I was, with a broken wing.

Daddy, I wanted to call out, *I broke my wing. Can you help me?*

Sometimes my imaginary friend and I played tic-tac-toe on those dusty stairs, and even kicked pebbles down, but nothing worked to get his attention.

On that cold and windy day, I went back upstairs, found my coat, and stomped out the door, sobbing and indignant.

AIR

Nature was my welcoming refuge. It was all around me and embraced me just as I was. Sometimes nature was dangerous, but I was drawn to it.

Hurricanes had always fascinated me, how they had the power to change the landscape. I felt excited at the end of every summer, wishing the powerful winds would blow the deadwood away and the world would start over fresh and new.

Hurricane Carol swept through southeastern Massachusetts in August of 1954. Ignoring my mother's warning, I ran out to the street where a huge tree had fallen down and was blocking traffic. Reaching up in the air, I grabbed at leaves the wind had prematurely separated from their branches.

Dancing around the street, I kept wishing the wind would carry me away and put me down, like it had Dorothy, far away from Kansas.

THE WOODS

Whether it was thirty degrees with two feet of snow on the ground or ninety degrees and humid, I learned to fashion a life for myself outdoors, usually in the woods.

Areas hollowed out by the wind became the rooms in my make-believe home fashioned on tree stumps and big granite boulders. Draping an old, tattered sheet over a low horizontal branch, I cut squares in it to make windows. Bits and pieces in the garage that had been left for the dump found new purpose in my imaginary home. Rusty tin cans, smashed under my feet, became ashtrays. An oversized bottle was turned into a lamp. A couple of old crates were repurposed as chairs. A broken old radio left near the brook added a nice touch to the kitchen table, itself a small scrap of plywood. Playing out my fantasies was a favorite pastime.

Inside the house, there was no escape. My family had moved into a converted schoolhouse in Massachusetts when I was six months old. There were four bedrooms upstairs, and since I was just a baby, my parents gave me the littlest one, the size of a large walk-in closet. As I grew, I felt terrible resentment toward my sister, Lucy, not only because she had been awarded the room with a window facing the lake and was a graceful dancing student but also because she was so much closer than I to our father. Still,

I tried tagging along with her, though I felt she didn't want me around.

One day I snuck into her room while Daddy was working in the basement and Mom was napping across the hall. *I could do anything!* I started by smashing one of her ballerina statues on the floor.

I looked at all her ballet costumes and pretty pink tutus. My sister was such a star, but I wanted attention too. I gazed at the perfumes and talcum powder on her dressing table. *Just for a little while, I can be a princess too.*

She had a growing collection of Joyce shoes, all carefully lined up in her closet. I just wanted to wear them in her room for a few minutes. I hoped that by putting on her shoes her magic would rub off on me. Maybe my parents would love me as much as they loved her.

I shuffled around, but the shoes were swimming on me as I struggled to keep them on my feet. So I gave up and put them back in her closet. Lucy would be home soon, and my princess time was running out. As I heard her approaching the stairs, I returned to my place in the corners of the house. Lucy went right into her closet.

I hadn't been careful to put the shoes back where they'd been neatly placed.

Why had I been so careless?

Exploding out of her room, Lucy confronted not me but our mother, who was awake by then, about my latest theft. Tears streaming down her face, she implored:

"Mother, Mary has been in my closet. She took my favorite shoes again. And she smashed my favorite ballerina on the floor. You always let her get away with this. Please *do* something this time!"

"Lucy, *you're* the older of the two of you. *You* do something."

What could my sister do? There was no justice to be found in our house.

Hiding in my little room with the door closed, I listened to my mother and sister. Eventually I left and went outside to my home in the woods. There I performed a mock trial.

Using one of my father's hammers, I banged my pretend gavel on a large granite boulder. "You know why you were bad, Mary," bellowed the judge. "You went into Lucy's room without permission. You wore her shoes. And you broke her statue. What do you have to say for yourself?"

"I just wanted to feel special. I thought if I put on her shoes, I'd feel special like she is. And I'm sorry I broke the ballet statue, but I'm so angry. Daddy loves her more than me!"

"That's not an excuse, Mary. There is no excuse for what you did."

"But I just wanted to get her attention!" I cried, breaking out in sobs.

The judge thundered back at me, unmoved, "You are guilty of jealousy and theft." *Guilty, guilty, guilty* . . .

Unable to convince the judge of my innocence, I went back inside the house, ran to my room, and slammed the door.

But I wasn't punished.

Guilty, guilty, guilty . . . those words buried themselves in a pocket next to my heart. And there they remained, like a ship's anchor, weighing me down for the rest of my life.

Mother busied herself making dinner, and my sister remained in her room. Invisible walls, unaddressed resentments, perpetual isolation.

From a very early age, I learned a terrible lesson: I could get away with things. If I were sneaky enough, or had enough enablers around me, my behaviors might yield no consequences. With no one slapping my wrist, the naughtiness continued. And my frustration and anger continued to chip away at my self-confidence and cloak itself in chronic depression.

I wasn't always a brat, though. Mother wrote in a diary entry dated 2/26/56:

> L and M quarreled, and I smacked them both. L stayed in her room and sulked. After a while M went into the kitchen, got out a plate of cookies, and poured a glass of milk. She carried up the cookies and on the way said to me, "I'm going to take these cookies up to Lucy and make her feel better."

STUFFING

Hugo, our mixed breed German shepherd, was warmhearted but not too bright. He acted like cats were dogs and slept with them in the big rocker on the side porch. One spring, our overbreeding cat, Herkimer, had just had her umpteenth litter, and the kittens were all nursing on the rocker. I came downstairs in the morning and couldn't wait to check on my new playmates. Two of them were flattened like pancakes. It was a frightful sight, and, as if to wipe it from my mind, I carried them out to the meadow to bury with a trowel.

Herkimer didn't seem to notice.

I had nowhere to go with my feelings. There was no place to express them safely in my family. But Mom liked it when we appreciated her cooking.

It was time for breakfast. Trying to escape from the horror I had just witnessed, I dug my hand into the big red cookie jar and wolfed down a bunch of her Toll House cookies. While she was making bacon and eggs, I returned to the meadow and made a cross out of twigs to put on the grave.

Herkimer and my mother had a lot in common. Both of them were overburdened by their circumstances and probably had too many children. Mom wasn't particularly sympathetic about Herkie's dead babies either.

"Oh, she'll have another litter next spring, Mary. You can be sure of that," she assured me, serving breakfast as I came inside, wiping my eyes. "Come sit down. Your eggs will get cold."

BLUEBERRIES

Our neighbor Sophie made the most mouthwatering blueberry pie. The crust was to die for, the way she sprinkled sugar into it as it baked. There was a blueberry meadow between our properties, and she lived on the lakeside in a large three-story house.

Sophie and her daughter, Martha, were alone at home, just the two of them. Sophie's husband was a doctor and was almost never home. He seemed like such a phantom to me. I remember seeing his car in the driveway once, but he was gone before I had a chance to pop in and get a look at him.

Someone told me that Sophie had had a stillborn son after Martha was born, and then there were no more children. Martha, who was my age, needed a playmate.

I spent a great deal of time with Martha there. We watched television on the sunporch facing the lake. Sometimes we played with dolls or we played board games. Martha was not an outdoorsy girl, so we always played inside. And I slept over often. Martha and I had the third floor all to ourselves. They really welcomed me into their family, and I relished being appreciated by them.

My mother didn't like the arrangement at all. She was jealous of the other family that had seduced me away from her. She didn't forbid me from going, but I remember the set of her jaw and her coldness toward me every time I did.

Sophie and her family were Jewish. She made Ashkenazi dishes often, and not just during the Jewish holidays. I raved to Mom once about Sophie's tasty matzo, or knaidel, balls, and she snapped, "I don't want to hear about Sophie's cooking anymore, Mary. Aren't I a good enough cook for you?"

But I didn't discriminate. I ate anything and everything that was put in front of me.

FAMILY TIES

Keeping animals in rural areas was easy. Dogs were allowed to go outside without a leash. One day, however, Hugo didn't come back. In addition to being pretty dumb, he was, apparently, gullible. That faithful, loving pet never would have run away on his own; I felt sure that he had been lured into a truck by dog snatchers, though my sister told me he'd been shot for pestering a female in heat up the road.

Teddy was another one of our dogs; he was bitten by a timber rattlesnake and died. We should have had Herkimer fixed; she had a litter just about every year until she was so worn out one day she just didn't wake up.

Corky was a beautiful Irish setter we got after Hugo disappeared. Arriving home from school one afternoon in fourth grade, I walked into the kitchen and found my mother sobbing at the kitchen table. This surprised me, if only because she usually hid her tears and sadness behind her closed bedroom door.

"Mommy, what's the matter?" I asked, approaching her and more afraid than usual when I saw her slip into that dark place.

"Oh, Mary!" she cried out, reaching for my hand. "I had to put Corky down this morning. He had a terrible ear infection, and there was nothing more the vet could do; the antibiotics weren't working. I just can't believe it. Such a waste of a beautiful dog."

"Oh no, Mommy!" I took her hand, looking around in vain for a sign of our dog, and burst into tears. Hugging each other then, we sobbed into each other's shoulders. Mother didn't steal away to her bedroom to cry, and I didn't go outdoors to be alone in the woods.

With perfect timing, Daddy came home from work early. He put his arms around my mother, genuinely sorry about Corky.

"Oh, Sid, I'm so glad you're home!" she cried, sobbing and falling into his arms.

For one afternoon, we gave up our isolation from one another. Losing Corky united us. Otherwise, it was an ordinary day for a family struggling under the hidden presence of alcoholism.

THE OLD MAN NEXT DOOR

An old man lived on the other side of our house through a thick grove of trees. His name was Mr. Schultz, and his wife had died. I walked by his house every day on my way to school and hoped to see him out front on his screened-in porch. Once, when I had seen him sitting there and waved, he got up and went back inside.

"Hi, Mr. Schultz," I called to him the next day as I walked past his house. The inside door closed behind him as he was about to sit in his rocker. But as soon as I called out to him, he turned around and went back inside.

Feeling rebuffed, I continued walking home. I was just trying to make a friend with someone close by. He seemed like a lonely old man, and I was lonely too. Maybe we could get together somehow. Maybe he could invite me in for cookies and milk on my way home.

But, as with my sister, my feelings of frustration quickly turned to anger.

One day I passed his house and before turning into my driveway, I opened his mailbox and took out the mail. The contents of one envelope looked like a check. I ripped it up and threw it in the brook across the street from our houses. Feeling no remorse, I was sure I would get away with it.

Weeks later, I found out Mr. Schultz had died. And I remember thinking, *It's my fault because I took his money away.*

COMET

B ill and I sailed on Lake Wampanoag, an old iron mine that
had been filled in as a reservoir two hundred years before we
lived near it. Sailing was my brother's great love, and he became
an expert sailor. At first Bill had a Comet, a sixteen-foot sloop
with a distinctively large mainsail. That worked well on a lake
with winds that were shifty. Later he had a big wooden Town
Class we named *Wind Song*. That wooden boat required a great
deal of maintenance work every year. I helped with the scraping
and painting; it was a real labor of love and one of the few opportunities I had to do something with him.

We had brought *Wind Song* over to the end of the lake near
our house to work on it.

"Mary, I need you to go home and get the clean brushes I left
near the back door. And ask Mom to find some rags and the jar
of turpentine near them. Hurry up because it's getting late and I
want us to finish this side today."

Running home from the lake, I tripped and fell, badly scraping my knees. I didn't care; I would have done anything to please
my brother.

Tabor Academy in Sippican Harbor was on Buzzards Bay,
where Bill could indulge his passion for sailing. Until vacations

and summer, when he came home, I sat on his bed in his empty room, looking for the piece of me that wasn't there anymore.

Ultimately, he joined the rest of the family members in shaking their heads, passing sorry looks all around, their hands up in the air, wondering what to do as I grew more and more troubled.

But my animals, whichever ones were left, still wagged their tails and were loyal.

Children in alcoholic families sometimes band together and support each other against a common enemy. But in other cases the children live in bubbles, isolated from one another, making their own way in life. Bill moved away, married, had a family, and I became a footnote, dutiful birthday cards sent in January.

SPONGE

Every summer our family spent time at the local yacht club where Bill's boat was moored near a swimming area.

One day I was hanging around the beach and became transfixed by profuse blood dripping from below a woman's knees. She was looking for a stick to pry bloodsuckers from her legs. One by one, they made a shriveled mess at her feet.

Lake Wampanoag was full of those little creatures. I decided to go swimming and stay in the water long enough to get some of my own on my legs. As soon as I came out of the lake, I ran to a spot in the woods for privacy. Counting two bloodsuckers on each calf, I watched them swell up.

Maybe they would suck all the evil out of me.

MANSIONS

Grammy had goldfish in the little pool off of the side porch. I was fascinated watching them—back and forth, back and forth, with nowhere to go.

They had nothing. And missed nothing.

Thanksgiving, Christmas, and Easter. Three holiday meals at Grammy's on Maplewood Avenue. Sometimes a maid served the meals. I never got her name. She'd already gone home when I hung out in the kitchen after the meal, pigging out from the fridge when no one was looking.

When I wasn't eating, I loved to play with the intercoms and chase my cousins around the third floor. Grumpy Uncle Ralph, Grammy's brother, hated all the noise. I peeked into his room once and saw all the empty bottles on the floor.

Sometimes I got to spend weekends there. I had my own room, down the hall from Aunt Pris, who had diabetes. I remember the insulin and the needle lying on her bedside table. I'd always been afraid of needles and admired her for being so brave, giving herself a shot every day.

My father had three sisters who doted on all their nieces and nephews. I loved them all so much, but Pris was special. She had married late and was freer in her twenties and thirties to spend time with her brother's children. She took me to the Isabella

Stewart Gardner Museum on the Fenway in Boston, and that's when I started getting curious about art and music. Aunt Pris nurtured a number of my interests, including sailing. Years later, after she married, she and my uncle would take us sailing with them on their boat every summer.

Once in the middle of the night, I wandered into Aunt Pris's bedroom. She slept in a single bed, and the room seemed small to me, almost like my bedroom back at my house.

"Aunt Pris, I can't sleep. Can I stay with you?"

"Let me walk you back to your bed, Mary Lee. You must be sleepwalking."

"Can I stay here and live with you?"

"Oh no, dear. Your mother and father would miss you terribly!" she responded, warmly hugging me as we reached my room.

"I don't think so, Aunt Pris," I argued, climbing back onto my bed. My aunt tucked me in and left right away, closing the door.

I spent the rest of the night staring at the ceiling, dreading the morning birds singing and the sound of my mother's car in the driveway.

NUT PIE

Wilbur didn't want food. He wanted love.

—E. B. White[4]

When I was a baby, I cried from hunger, and someone fed me. Later, when I was able to talk, I asked for food.

Craning my neck upward while my mother was cooking at the stove, I fussed, "I'm hungry, Mommy."

So my mother gave me something to eat.

I escaped from my house by going outdoors all the time, winter or summer. In addition to walking back and forth to school a mile every day, I sledded down the hill behind the Unitarian church, dragging my sled back up. The lake provided ice skating in the winter and swimming in the summer. In spite of all this activity, I grew chubby.

At the end of Lake Wampanoag closest to my house, there were fewer bloodsuckers and there was a food stand on each end of the beach. Stationing myself in the middle, I wouldn't have to walk very far to eat. And it seemed like I was eating all the time.

But Mom didn't worry about it until I was a teenager. By then I was already a food addict, and there was very little she could do to control my eating. She could put her finger in the dike here and there, but she had no idea what she was dealing with. Substance use awareness was in its infancy back then.

Mother jotted down this little jingle that she said I wrote when I was five years old:

I have a little nut pie.
Would you like to take it home?
Oh yes, I would, oh yes, I would.
Could I eat it all alone?

Everyone who read it chuckled. "Oh, that's cute. Mary Lee likes to eat!"

The passage of time, like the panoramic setting on a camera, lends perspective to the events in my life, and I can see more now. Despite her preoccupations, my mother was often remarkably caring and attentive when it came to writing down words I'd said.

Once in the middle of the night, Mother transcribed a bad dream I must have tearfully recounted to her:

2/1/53: "Something disappears and twirls into twinkles. Partly I hear a lot of tiptoes every night, and I hear a little bit of noise on a foot stair. A wolf turns twinkles into her eyebrows. I thought maybe this house was a ghost house because it didn't look like it was a real family's house; it looked just like a ghost house. There were a couple of curtains gone, and that looked just like a ghost house or a wolf house."

I didn't feel embraced or valued there.
I lived in a wolf house and was afraid all the time.

CHANGING TIMES

My father, and his father before him, graduated from Harvard University. Many of our relatives studied there, and Daddy was proud of the Harvard tradition in our family. We all celebrated the twenty-fifth reunion of the Class of '34 on the Harvard campus in 1959.

Daddy's family had a successful business in Boston, and he worked there for a few years. But it didn't work out for him, and he decided to strike out on his own. He started a business renting televisions and radios to a couple of hospitals in the area where we lived. By 1954, 50 percent of the households in our country had television, and it was good business for my father to bring it to patients in hospitals.

Wherever we lived, Daddy always made sure we had several televisions. That seemed like quite a luxury to me. Later on in my own apartment, he always spoiled me with one. I had an old Philco for a long time and hated to toss it when the picture tube burned out.

He was proud of what he did for a living. Mother economized in every possible way and earned money herself wherever she could. Pulling together as a team when it came to making ends meet, they both worked hard to see that we never lacked for material things.

THE SUB

Irma Jackson, my favorite teacher, taught fifth grade. At nearly six feet tall, she towered over all of us. She was a powerful giant in my eyes, and I wanted to be a good student to win my mother's approval. I worked extra hard to learn my multiplication tables because I needed those As on my report card.

That year, I couldn't wait to go to school. As soon as I crossed the threshold, I scanned the room for her; she was always somewhere working. When she saw me, she dropped what she was doing and made me the focus of her attention. She saw something in me that would take me decades to discover: an intelligence, someone of value, someone worth nurturing.

Mrs. Jackson helped me trust my abilities. How does one do that? How does a skilled teacher embolden a child, taking her on a winged victory ride to the transformation even a tiny success can bring? She had that kind of talent, and though I filed it away and would lose it time and again, that confidence stayed buried within me all my life.

My fifth-grade class was in charge of decorating the display case next to the main office for the Christmas holidays. Mrs. Jackson put me in charge of the project. We made a facsimile of stained glass. There were three glass panels to fill, and I elected to do a manger scene in the center with an angel in each of the side panels.

I created the template, and the class all had their own tasks: using reams of colored paper provided by the art department, one group cut out yellow angel wings; another group followed my template to cut out the angels' gowns; a third group cut out the lambs in white and the manger scene in colors of their choosing.

It all came together, and we carefully taped the pieces of the scene to the inside of the three panes of glass. All three sections of the display case had electrical outlets, so we could place a low-wattage bulb in the background and illuminate the scene. It was an ordinary Christmas scene, evocative of much of our culture in the United States in 1958. I went home to enjoy Christmas vacation, feeling proud of myself for undertaking such a successful school project.

The day we went back to school, I learned that Mrs. Jackson had had a ski accident and would be recuperating at home for the rest of the school year. But my disappointment was eclipsed by sheer mortification when I found out that my mother would be substituting for her.

As our class was being informed of this unwelcome surprise, I felt the color leaving my face. The cold stares of twenty-one fifth graders pummeled me one by one, then seemingly all at once. I heard the snickering and felt them pulling away, as though I'd suddenly become another life form. The walls seemed to close in on me and I froze, gazing at the icicles hanging from the gutters outside the window.

Oh, no! Ten years old, fat, awkward, and now I had to both loathe and defend my own mother.

We lived comfortably, but Mother occasionally substituted in the public schools in our town. Though money had been tight during the Depression, she graduated from New York University, not a small accomplishment. Later on, she studied developmental reading and she worked in that field for a little while, but she didn't stay at it. She'd always wanted to be a teacher, and subbing was a way to get into the classroom.

Mother was nearly fifty at the time, with blue-gray hair. That was the rinse women used back in the 1950s to cover the gray. But she looked silly to me then with that odd color in her hair. She had just gotten a perm, and her head was a nest of tightly woven spirals that she clipped together to stay in place.

School had been another refuge for me. The one reason I loved to go to school was so I could get away from that house and try to shine somewhere—the reason why Saturday was the saddest day of the week but Sunday was more bearable because I had school to look forward to. Now, and for the rest of the school year, my school would become a prison.

A snowstorm was starting to blow in as I was walking home from school. The sky was getting darker to match my mood, and thick wet flakes were starting to fill the air. Without a hat, I hurried home, stopping short when I saw my mother's car in the driveway. Melting snowflakes all over my face disguised my tears, but I didn't waste any time confronting her. Hurrying through the front door, I saw that she was in the kitchen taking her Toll House cookies out of the oven.

"Mommy, are you really going to teach my class for the rest of the year?" I asked, my face hot with tears and indignation. "Some of the kids are already making fun of me. Jimmy called me 'Mama's Girl' at the lunch table."

In need of sympathy and a hug, all I detected was her resolve.

"Mary," she said, dismissing me, "you're making too much of this. With Bill away at college, I need to do what I can to pitch in."

"But why does it have to be my class? Why can't Mrs. Jackson come back? We could all help her carry her things." Seeing her jaw tighten as she loosened the cookies from the tray, breaking a couple, I tried one more time. "Please, Mommy, can't you teach another class?"

Growing impatient with all my questions, she snapped, "No! This opportunity just came up, and I don't want to turn it away." She turned her back to me, putting up a wall. Then, hearing me crying, she turned around and added, "It'll be fine, Mary. You'll be my helper in the classroom."

But no hug.

The cookies had just come out of the oven and smelled good. I grabbed a handful of them and poured myself a glass of milk. Mother didn't notice what I was doing to stuff my feelings. When she was sad, she closed herself off and stayed in her bedroom. But I'd defaulted to food ever since I could remember. It filled up the empty spaces, and it comforted me. "Okay," I said, defeated.

There was a little shed on the side of the garage that I used, another outside place in addition to my home in the woods for my friends and me. It still had a dirt floor, but it was mine.

I went out there to be alone and stood on the dirt floor with the red roll-top desk behind me, imagining what it would be like with my mother as my teacher. I fantasized all kinds of scenarios: scenes of my mother scowling and kids sneering at her; scenes of me smacking Jimmy for making fun of her, then pretending to be sick for days at a time so I didn't have to go to school; scenes of me hugging my mother and then running away from her.

For the nearly six months that she taught my class, I felt painfully isolated among most of my peers. Longing to be one of the gang, I was on the outside of my peer group because I was the teacher's daughter, a strange place that suggested a privilege I never asked for.

When students made fun of her, loudly, flamboyantly, I felt so torn, so conflicted, alternately ashamed to be her daughter and loyal to her. Furious with many of the other kids, I was mad at my mother, too, for putting me in that uncomfortable position.

Totally powerless to control the situation, I suffered through it like I endured getting drilled without novocaine by the most sadistic dentist in town. There was no escape from that either.

HEAVEN
OR HELL?

I f it hadn't been for my best friend, Juliette, I would have been
  completely isolated. She lived on the same street as our elementary school, and most days we walked to school together. Her
house was just three blocks away, on the other side of the Catholic
church. She was a devout Catholic and told me that Catholicism
was the only true religion. Of course I believed her. I was feeling
so ostracized at school, and grateful that I still had Julie for a
friend, that I was easily seduced by her strong religious conviction. I felt I'd better try to fit into her world since the foundation
of mine was so shaky.

"Aren't you afraid of going to hell, Mary?" she asked, turning
to face me with a penetrating look. I envisioned myself burning
for all eternity.

As we walked past Our Lady of Assumption Catholic Church
on the way to school every day, I paused to look at the statue of the
Virgin Mary. She wore such a sad expression because she had lost
her son. I wasn't happy because I didn't know where I belonged. I
kept attaching myself to other people, looking for acceptance, all
the while envying Juliette for the closeness of her family and for
finding peace in something so much greater than herself. I felt

so alone in my house: Bill wasn't home much, Lucy had other interests, and my parents were distant. So I delved into my family church visits every Sunday.

Ours was a high Episcopal church, which was close to Catholicism. I loved all the ritual, learned all the hymns, and can still recite the Nicene Creed by heart. I particularly liked communion Sundays and going up to the railing for a wafer. Our minister didn't offer me a sip of wine, but I made the sign of the cross like Juliette had showed me, pretending to be Catholic in my own church.

Juliette and I went to Stations of the Cross at her church every Friday during Lent. Then we ate tomato soup and tuna sandwiches at my house. No meat on Fridays, and not just during Lent.

My mother humored me through all this. She viewed it as a phase that would pass.

Julie had to go home, but I watched *The Wizard of Oz* on my father's newest television set in our family room. My favorite character was the Cowardly Lion. I'd wished I could have been brave like he was in the end. But I wasn't brave. I concealed my fear behind bravado, recklessness, and the appearance of not caring—when I wasn't outright depressed and alone in my bedroom.

That year Juliette and I entered a science fair together, busily working on "Tides and Currents," which won first prize.

Running over to Juliette's house, I was breathless with good news. "Julie, Mrs. Jackson told Mom our project has won first prize! I'm so excited. Aren't you proud?"

"Yeah, wow, I was sure James would win with all those papier-mâché animals. We just had posters, but oh, yes, we did have the 3-D model."

"Well, Mrs. Jackson said we won because we explained everything so well to the judges, like we knew what we were talking about."

"We did, Mary! We grilled each other every day. Anyway, you can keep it because we've started packing for the move, and Mom said I need to start throwing out stuff."

All the boxes in her living room suddenly loomed in importance. As soon as she mentioned moving, I felt the breath leave my body for a moment.

"Julie, who was your favorite character in *The Wizard of Oz?*" I had asked her after she'd seen the movie too. "I bet it was Glinda. She knew how to save Dorothy."

"No, I really liked the Tin Man. I thought it was funny how he was always afraid of crying because he'd get rusty. But we need to cry sometimes, don't we?"

Juliette had a big heart and was loyal. She remained my friend even when some of my classmates were turning away from me. As much as I loved anyone, I loved Julie. When she and her family moved away, saddened to say goodbye to my best friend, I folded into myself in my little bedroom.

APPEARANCES

After I turned twelve and had a certain amount of independence, I escaped from my house beyond the woods as much as possible, sometimes on an airplane. Mom and Dad happily sent me places.

My first trip away from my family was to Florida to visit my aunt Dodie and uncle Geo after they'd been married for about nine years.

Geo (George) was dark and swarthy, a movie star handsome hunk of a man, and he adored my aunt Dodie. His arms found their way all over her, and I can see why because she always smelled terrific, as though she'd bathed in rose petals. I sat next to her and watched as she pressed cake makeup onto her face every morning.

She's so pretty. No wonder Uncle Geo loves her so much!

"Aunt Dodie," I started, timid about asking. "Can you show me how to put that on?"

"Why sure, darling." She picked up her compact, pressing a small amount of the makeup on my nose and cheeks.

Wow, what a difference! My freckles and moles are lighter! At not yet thirteen, I decided then and there to start wearing cake makeup.

I had been a terrible nail biter before and during puberty.

But when Dodie got one look at my nails, chewed up like a wild animal's, her jaw dropped. She doused my nails in vinegar and put me in some white gloves that I hated but, in spite of the heat, I put up with. I loved the way she cared about me. For the two weeks that I was there, my nails grew out just enough for her to file them a little, straighten them out; then she showed me how to paint them.

After returning to my parents' house, I started wearing cake makeup to school. I looked cheap and started to behave cheaply as well. I felt I had little value. My seventh-grade teacher, a mean, snarky old woman, called me up to her desk one morning and, grim-faced as though she'd caught me cheating on a quiz, showed me where I'd missed a spot on my cheek just below my left eye. She wasn't being helpful, just shaming and judging me. That wounded me deeply.

Mother was dismayed by the makeup routine following my return from Florida. And so, her face pinched in disapproval as I left for school, she made sure I never went to Florida again. I was furious with her for cutting me off from two people who loved me and really enjoyed having me around.

ATTICS

I heard my aunt calling up the back stairs, and her voice was full of accusation. "What are you two doing up there? Come back down here. We'll be eating soon."

I looked down at the base of the stairs. She had a drink in her hand, and she sounded angry. Her tone stung me.

My cousin and I came back downstairs. We were both twelve and we weren't doing anything they'd disapprove of, but I felt cheap anyway.

SCREAMS

*From early infancy onward we all incorporate
into our lives the message we receive concerning our
self-worth, or lack of self-worth, and this message is
to be found beneath our actions and feelings as
a tangled network of self-perception.*

—Christina Baldwin[5]

"Well, you're a young lady now," Mother informed me matter-of-factly as I told her about the blood in my underpants.

Her tone was as cramped as I was beginning to feel, my menstruating just another glaring reminder that humans were sexual beings, something she would have liked to forget. But she was ready for me and went into her bureau drawer and found a couple of pamphlets she asked me to read. She'd already been through this with my sister, and once again, I was left to my own devices to figure things out.

It was 1961 when puberty ignited in me like a wildfire. I became utterly boy crazy. Thus began my quest to explore my sexuality in the most inappropriate ways, ways that would guarantee my place in the frozen outer circle of not fitting in among my peers.

In seventh grade, when I heard my name had appeared prominently in the boys' locker room, I knew I was in demand by the opposite sex! Ever since Bill had moved away, I'd felt abandoned in my house, and I continued to feel more and more dismissed by my father. I was vulnerable and lonely, and didn't have any of the essential boundaries I needed to recognize and avoid promiscuity. Instead of running in the opposite direction, I walked right into the hornet's nest when I found a small envelope taped to my locker door. "Meet me at 4:00 tomorrow on the other side of the brook across from your house. I just want to talk."

It was a dark, drizzly January day, but awaiting me was an invitation to feel wanted, at least for a little while, so I showed up. The boy I knew from seventh grade was there along with his older brother and other high school juniors—about six boys.

And me.

Did I feel deceived that he had misled me into thinking he would be coming alone?

No. I felt flattered that all those boys wanted to see me.

"You're so beautiful, Marilea," the thirteen-year-old said to me. "Would you take off your shirt and bra so we can see your breasts?"

I complied.

All I remember is the swipe of a boy's dirty fingernail across my still-undeveloped right breast.

Next, I recall sitting in the big stuffed chair in my living room, staring out at the street for hours. Clocks stopped ticking, rain stopped dripping from the gutters, and I stopped moving. I just sat in the chair paralyzed, staring out at the street, collapsing inward like an accordion.

My brother was away, my sister was busy with her friends, and Daddy was working on his radios. But I did something that successfully got my mother's attention.

I sat on the stoop in front of our laundry line, took a piece of glass, and slit one of the veins on the outside of my right wrist. I ran to get a rag in the kitchen to stop the bleeding, but instead of hiding in my bedroom, I went back to the stoop and called out to my mother. As she approached, I held out my wrist with the bloody rag absorbing the blood. This was as close to screaming as I could get at that point in my life.

"Mary! My God, what have you done?" She looked stricken. By then Mother had been living under a lot of stress for twenty-five years, and she knew little about self-care. Her solution was taking to her bed, anger, manipulation, and staying in control. Now it looked like she was facing something too big for her, and she was frightened.

Trying to minimize the situation, my instinct was to protect her. "I'm sorry, Mom. I stupidly slipped and fell on a piece of glass outside. Don't worry. I just thought I might need stitches. But it's stopped bleeding, so I guess not."

In addition to getting away with things, I had also learned to be a good liar. This is what she wanted to hear, so she buried the matter, and I don't believe she ever told my father. Nothing was resolved—just more family dysfunction buried under the rug.

A couple of weeks later, I made another not-so-covert attempt to communicate to my mother what I'd been doing in my spare time.

I made a list in two columns on a piece of paper: "Reasons to Stay Here" and "Reasons to Move." In the "Reasons to Move" column, I wrote, "My Reputation," and I left this list where Mother would find it. My mother had a mania for appearances. Inside our family, serious problems, like my depression, were minimized—at times outright ignored.

When, as I'd predicted, she confronted me, I tearfully told her that I was indeed unhappy in that town and wanted to move away.

As though my sadness came from the outside and had nothing to do with what had been happening inside our family. Again, that is what she wanted to hear. Lacking the tools to manage both her marital situation and a daughter who was spinning out of control, she felt terribly overwhelmed herself and, as many people do, hoped for a geographical cure.

Mother spent some of the happiest times of her life on Long Island, outside of New York City. Her parents had a summer home two blocks from the water, where she and her sister went swimming often, sometimes at night when the current might have pulled them under, but they didn't care. That's how much they needed to get away and let the sea swallow them up for a while.

She'd been accustomed to the smell of salt from the ocean and missed it when we moved to Massachusetts from New Jersey. A beautiful home near the sea was what she had wanted for a long time. When Dad finally agreed to move closer to the salt water, she was in heaven. Plans to relocate that summer to a more socially prominent town had been set in motion.

My mother would find out soon enough that moving away did nothing to slow down the locomotive in front of her.

DETOUR

After that January encounter in the woods, I thought boys were horrid and ungrateful. Instead of burning up my phone line, they ran off with pretty blond cheerleaders who played hard to get and teased their balls blue. I felt used and abused, and my sexual awakening took off in another direction. I fell in love with Pamela. She became my new best friend, and we were inseparable.

Her family rented the upper level of a large Victorian house near the lake, and I was a frequent visitor. The aromas of toasted *guajillos* and cilantro seduced me as I walked through the door for lunch most Saturdays. Her Mexican mother made the most mouthwatering chilaquiles, and I often hung around late enough after school to get an impromptu dinner invitation as well. They had six kids in the family, and one more was always welcome.

One spring weekend when my sister was away, Pamela came for a sleepover. Since my room had a single bed, we had permission to sleep in Lucy's bedroom. The ensuing comedy is one for the books. We were passionate about each other; I loved her wide, round mouth and the little buds on her chest that started to fill out her training bra.

We spent the night naked in my sister's big double bed trying to make love to each other. I remember two flat and mildly fuzzy vaginas rubbing against each other, and though neither of us seemed to know the nuts and bolts of sex between our parents, we did know that something fundamental was missing.

Though Pamela and I preferred boys after our encounter, we remained steadfastly in love for several months after I moved away. We wrote long, passionate letters back and forth until I developed a crush a year later on a boy in my new town.

THE HOUSE
BY THE LAKE

That summer I said goodbye to the house where I'd lived since I was six months old. My mother never drove me back to see any of my friends, not even Pamela.

I'd call random numbers on the phone and listen to whomever answered.

"It's your money," they'd growl before they hung up. I did that a lot. My parents' phone bill must have been huge.

But they never said anything.

Except for a spate of letters from Pamela, and occasional letters and cards from Juliette over the years, I've hardly communicated with anyone in that town since moving away.

I disconnected myself, like all those phone calls to people I didn't know.

NEW KID

Jumping into adolescent endeavors at thirteen, I rode the highs and lows that went with being a teenager. Starting yo-yo dieting with the onset of puberty, I was in one of my "thin" periods, attractive and noticed right away at the new school.

In order to ingratiate myself with my new friends, I had a Make Out Party (MOP) at my house. My new boyfriend was there with me, and that was the beginning and the end of our relationship.

We lay horizontally on my mother's camelback sofa in the darkness. It was a warm evening, and half the couples were outside necking in the bushes. I heard their beer cans being kicked around. My parents were upstairs in their bedroom, either asleep or pretending to be. They never came downstairs to turn on the lights.

Busy hungrily kissing my new boyfriend, my appetite must have overwhelmed him, so much so that he didn't know what to do with me—or perhaps with his own awakening sexuality. Being a nice boy from the right side of town, he decided that I wasn't a nice girl from the right side of town. On Monday morning at school, I heard snickering in the halls and the circulating rumor that I was a sex maniac. Nowadays we know that spreading those kinds of rumors is a form of sexual harassment. But in those days, who knew?

Looking back, it was probably a fair conclusion for a thirteen-year-old boy to draw under the circumstances. I was nevertheless so enraged by his callousness—this was the boy I dumped Pamela for?—that I threw the copper heart he had made me into the woods behind my house.

I spent a whole afternoon at the end of the summer—before the leaves had started to fall—searching for it. Looking under every fallen branch, I even braved the edge of the cliff our house was sitting on, hoping the sun would reflect the coppery shine, but no luck.

I had quite a temper.

GATHERING
STEAM

"Young lady, turn around. Let me see the bag you're carrying," ordered the salesclerk, grim and resolute. Hoping I'd earn points by fessing up to my crime, I took the record out of my shopping bag and handed it to her.

"I'm so sorry," I lamented, breaking down and sobbing in the record department.

I spent hours at our house listening to LPs in the living room. Mantovani was a composer known for his use of strings, one of the most emotional instruments in musical composition. Another favorite was Rod McKuen. He set some of his poetry to music, with the San Sebastian Strings in the background. I lost myself in the music and McKuen's poems, mostly contemplative and often sad, and had amassed quite a collection of LPs in my teens.

One or two of them were stolen. On occasion I continued to seek the thrill of taking something that wasn't mine, and on this day at the department store, I got caught.

"Please, please, please, let me just give it back. I'm so sorry. I don't know what got into me. I would have paid for it before I left the store because I know it's wrong to steal. Please, don't call the police. My mother would absolutely kill me. You have no idea. I would want to die if she found out. Can you please let me leave? I feel so terrible. Believe me, I'll never do it again. I'm begging you, give me a chance to learn my lesson."

I saw the misgivings in her eyes. She must have known the only lesson I would learn was that I could get away with things if I were lucky.

"All right," she said, resigned to her decision. "I hope you are sufficiently scared and will remember this incident. Don't you ever come into this store again!"

Racing away from the store, I felt almost elevated, and giddy with relief. The rush of coming close to disaster and skirting it was becoming a pattern in my life. The more I got away with things, the more risks I wanted to take.

SUNLIGHT

Sometimes survival is as simple as saying yes instead of no. At fifteen, I'd been working in a volunteer position for two months.

Mom knew I was sad and that I needed a distraction, a positive activity that would free me of my self-absorption. So she drove me over to the home for blind people every Saturday.

There was one visit when I came away smiling.

After she dropped me off, I went around the back and walked down to the marsh. A beautiful heron was standing behind a clump of reeds. When I approached, he flew away, squawking loudly.

Harold was an old man who didn't want to leave his room except for meals. He never went outside. My supervisor introduced us while he was eating lunch in the dining room. Sitting down with him, I asked if he wanted to listen to the Met after lunch. He said no.

It was a sunny day. I asked him if he'd enjoy a walk. He said no.

I asked him if he'd like me to read to him in his room. He said no.

To keep him company, I ate a bowl of ice cream while he enjoyed his apple pie.

"Marilea, is that your name?" he asked, looking in my direction and warming up to me. "What a pretty name."

"Thanks, Harold. I made it up. It's not my real name. My real name is Mary Lee, but I didn't like it, so I changed the spelling."

"Good for you! A brave thing to do!"

"You think so? Well, I just want to be someone else."

"Why?"

"Cuz I don't like who I am."

"Oh, let's not open that can of worms!"

"Okay," I agreed, a little embarrassed.

Harold finished his pie and just sat there, looking in my direction.

"Harold," I said, starting to get up, "the path from the patio outside leads down to a marsh. Standing at the edge earlier, I saw a heron. And then I could hear an egret croaking before it flew away. Do you like to listen to the birds around here? Some of them are so noisy. My mother has a record of bird calls she likes to listen to."

"Oh, yes. Some days that's all I do. My room is on the marsh side, and I can hear the noises at night."

"Do they keep you awake?"

"No, I'm used to them by now," he answered, getting to his feet.

"It's a little chilly outside, but the sun feels warm today. Mom's picking me up in an hour." I repeated my earlier invitation. "You wanna go down to the marsh before I go?"

"Marilea. Such a pretty name."

"Thanks, Harold." I steadied him with my hand. "Let me walk you back to your room."

"Sure, Marilea. My coat is there. I might need my hat today too."

MUSIC

What most of us want is to be heard,
to communicate.

—Dory Previn[6]

So I sang. But I was so shy and self-conscious that I lost my voice from stage fright the night in high school when I was to sing the alto solo.

My singing teacher, Mr. Bianchi, had coached me every day after school; he knew me pretty well and wanted to ease my anxiety.

That evening, the chorus sang beautifully. But when I opened my mouth and formed the words, no sound came out. Was it fear of failure that paralyzed my vocal chords?

Poor Mr. Bianchi didn't know what to do except move ahead to the next piece. No doubt my solo career would be over.

But my father, who loved music and listened to recordings incessantly, felt I was such a good alto that he encouraged me to try out for a statewide singing competition.

Breathless from running, I entered the garage to his back room.

"Daddy! I made it! All-State accepted me. We're performing in the spring, and there will be an album of all the music!" I raved, gushing and desperate for his approval.

"Well," he deadpanned, "you certainly are your father's daughter." My confidence momentarily restored by acceptance into the All-State Festival Concert, I enjoyed a few years of choral singing, proud to be contributing to the musical tradition in my family.

We heard music in our house all the time—from Louis Armstrong to Handel. Mother spent many Saturdays listening to operas broadcast from the Met in New York. Growing up in New Jersey, that's what she had done with her family. There was no television then, just books and music. My mother passed a love of opera on to me.

My sister went on to sing madrigals in college. And my brother, the most talented, sang barbershop tenor for over fifty years. He made numerous albums, and in recent years he has mentored young people as well.

Beautiful music helped us withstand the day-to-day stresses of alcoholism that, back in the 1960s, was a silent and invisible predator.

AMBITION

"So, Marilea," a middle-aged, bald interviewer for the American Field Service asked, "you say here on the application that you enjoy reading the *New York Times*. What do you think of Scotty Reston?"

Silence.

My face was as blank as a snowy landscape in Alaska. Frozen in my chair, I felt my confidence plummet.

He politely moved on to another question, and the committee mercifully dispatched me quickly.

I'm sure I was not the first high school student to embellish an application with impressive intellectual feats. But I had lied shamelessly, and this time there were consequences.

The day I received confirmation that I hadn't made the final cut from semi to finalist, I crawled up the driveway.

"Daddy," I called out as I saw him in the garage. "I didn't make finalist. I wanted it so badly." I continued walking up to him and fell into his arms.

"There, there. It's okay. I'm still proud of you," he said, patting my back.

In that brief moment, my father was everything I'd ever needed him to be.

A REFRIGERATOR
HALF-FULL

This travel charm is somewhat late.
They all were trite flat discs of plate.
And then behold this I did spy,
For our young traveler, I did buy
This charming globe with continents, all seven
Hope in France it'll be just like heaven.
Poetic license I do claim
And pray forgive, the poetry's lame.

—Mother, 1965

Mom and Dad signed me up for Vacances Studieuses that summer. I wouldn't be an exchange student from my high school, but this program would allow me to travel. One of many language enrichment programs available to kids who wanted to learn another language, it was an excellent opportunity to get to know not only the French language but also the culture as well. I would be living not in a dormitory with other Americans but with a French family. The families selected all spoke fluent English. This facilitated communication, but it became a crutch for some kids who were lazy about practicing French.

My host family lived in a tiny village several miles from Bourges, a town in central France famous for its Gothic cathedral. Driving into the village, I seemed to be in a time warp—just one winding street with all the shops and old crumbling buildings. That was my first taste of rural continental Europe, and I had much to learn about differing cultures and the changing rhythms of life.

Like most European women, my French mother went shopping every day: to the butcher for meat, the baker for bread, and the vegetable and fruit stands. There was no shopping plaza, no Stop & Shop or other large food store. Everything was bought fresh and eaten that day. It was a healthy way to eat and time-consuming. But women in that village had little work outside the home, not unless they were shopkeepers. Their lives revolved around their families.

When I arrived at the farmhouse of Madame and Monsieur Pelletier, their grown children, Simone and Jacques, were away for the summer, so I would be the only child in the house. I would quickly see, on my tour around before dinnertime, that the only food in the house was what we were about to eat. No chips staying crisp in the oven, no cookies or a cake, no freezer full of ice cream—no freezer at all—just a small refrigerator with milk, butter, a few eggs, and a moldy carrot. No condiments, mayonnaise, cold cuts, nothing that looked familiar to me.

There wasn't even any bread in the house. That was bought fresh every morning and was meant to serve three people, not just me. The butter was not there for me to slather all over it; it was used for cooking just about everything: *sautéed haricots verts, sautéed pommes de terre, la viande.* That wasn't enough food for me. Where was all the junk food I craved? How was I going to take care of my gastronomical needs in that little farmhouse?

After a few days of no snacking, I started to fantasize that I was Scarlett O'Hara, dirty fingernails and all, holding a newly foraged carrot over her head and swearing to God: "I'll never be hungry again!"

Uh-huh . . .

Well, after two weeks of eating just three meals a day, I couldn't stand it anymore. I wasn't even hungry; food addiction is something quite apart from that. And though I had been a food addict all my life, this was the first time I was about to be confronted with my malady.

In other words, there would be a witness, and that would make it real.

Waking up in the middle of the night, just shooting up to a sitting position, I felt the troll approaching. The troll was my evil twin, that ugly and powerful creature that encouraged my insane binges. And I always let him in—I never said go away.

Hoping Madame and Monsieur were sound sleepers, I snuck downstairs to the kitchen and opened the refrigerator. There they were, leftovers from dinner: some pommes frites, a few haricots verts, and three mouthwatering sausage links, all cooked and ready to devour.

How do I describe the mind of a food addict about to pounce on her prey, or about to shoot up a substance that promises oblivion for a few moments? We lose all sense of reason, focusing only on the result.

And we often get careless.

I didn't pay attention to the round-bottomed pitcher of milk leaning against the plate of potatoes that I yanked out of the refrigerator. The pitcher toppled forward, spilling onto the few things that were there. Unable to catch it before it landed on the cold kitchen floor, I watched as it shattered into big ceramic shards that needed to be picked up along with the milk. Rolling my eyes, I knew the noise would wake Madame.

I froze in astonishment, amazed that I could be so careless and allow myself to be discovered in the kitchen in the middle of the night. Of course, I wasn't thinking it through anyway. How was I planning to explain the missing food the next day? Like all tried and true addicts, we just want what we want when we want it.

Delayed gratification? What's that?

As my mind raced to come up with an explanation, I heard Madame coming downstairs.

"*Marie, que fais-tu?*" She stared at the broken pitcher and spilled milk on the floor in front of the open refrigerator door.

I just looked at her, speechless.

"*As-tu faim?*" was the only logical question she could think of.

"*Oui, Madame. J'avais très faim.* I'm so sorry," I lied, and started crying, so embarrassed to have been discovered raiding her refrigerator in the middle of the night.

Madame was one of the kindest women I'd ever known. She had earlier prepared a delicious dinner for us all; she knew I wasn't really hungry. But what else did she know? Young women in that little farming village in the middle of France were not likely to be prone to eating disorders. In any case, intuitive and nurturing as she was, my French mother could see how troubled I was but that all I needed in that moment was an arm around my shoulder as she accompanied me back to bed.

Sitting beside me, her arms falling loosely in her lap, she started to talk in a sad, faraway voice about her life twenty-three years before, in 1942. I felt transported back in time as she recalled how hard it was for so many of the French during the German occupation, how the Nazis took all the good food for themselves while many of the French were starving. Coming from a land of so much abundance, I couldn't imagine what that had been like.

"Marie," she told me, taking my hands in her own, "most Americans have much luck to not know the miseries of war in their own land. I was a young wife with a son and daughter when the Germans occupied France. *J'avais vraiment peur tous les jours.*"

Oh, I'm feeling so ashamed, I thought, looking down at the floor. *She must have been so afraid*. Then I quickly returned her gaze and listened as she continued:

"We had ration cards for food, and if we're not in the queue early in the morning, there is no more food for us. We maybe have to wait another day to eat. It's good Monsieur is a good farmer and grew in secret some vegetables behind the barn. But many days we were hungry, and Simone cried from the pain in her stomach."

Able now to articulate my thoughts, I said, "Oh, Madame, I feel so ashamed. I don't think I've ever really been hungry a day in my life. I don't understand why I do the crazy things I do sometimes, but thank you for being so nice to me tonight!"

"No, *ce n'est rien*, Marie, don't worry," she said, reassuring me.

There was no judgment in her voice, no condemnation of my erratic behavior. Just a desire to show me another perspective, her own personal one, on the value of food in life: just the source of sustenance we all need, nothing more, nothing less.

That simple woman showed me exactly what I needed in that moment of frailty. Bolstered by her unconditional acceptance of me, I had no trouble feeling satisfied by the three meals a day we shared. The troll banished for the time being, I was able to appreciate what was right in front of me.

MANISCHEWITZ

D addy often came home from the corner liquor store with a present for me: Manischewitz grape wine.

I can see him in the kitchen now, excitedly taking the bottle out of a brown paper bag, hoping to find a drinking buddy. My mother was no fun in that department: she could nurse a glass of sherry for five hours.

So he turned to me. I might have been closer to him if I'd climbed into his gin bottle with him. But I hated hard liquor in those days and hardly drank at all. The grape wine was like soda pop with a kick.

What I remember was his loneliness. How he often stumbled up to his bed, closed the curtains, and shielded his eyes from the light. From my room next to his, I could hear him groaning from the migraines he was experiencing.

I never hated my father.

It was my mother I hated—for not loving him enough.

PROM DRESS

In my senior year after my return from France, I often drove to the beach after school with my girlfriend in her convertible. My reputation had been tarnished in junior high, so almost all of my high school boyfriends had come from the town next to ours. And the beach in that town is where I met Preston. He and I fell hard for each other. My old friend Juliette would have been proud: Preston was Catholic.

We dated all year, and both of us applied to first-class colleges. Wheaton College and Connecticut College accepted me. I went to two senior proms with Preston—at his school and at mine—in a beautiful gown that my mother made; I had my long hair pulled up in the back and fashioned into a bun held by a hairpiece. Mother had also made a cape to go with the gown, and the two of us were a handsome pair. We were very much in love, and that added a magnificent glow.

Preston chose Princeton, and I picked Wheaton since it was closer to home. I needed to get farther away, but I was still in a love-hate struggle with my own independence—and my mother.

CAVING

"Hey, Marilea," my pizza parlor coworker Pete called over to me as I was taking an order at a table, "isn't that your mother over there talking to the manager? They don't look happy." Smirking openly, he was enjoying my discomfort. Pete worked there because he had to, because his father and mother could barely pay the rent on their house by the railroad tracks—not without the help of their five children pitching in. He knew I didn't need the summer work, and he resented my being there when one of his sisters could have been earning my paycheck.

Please, God, tell me I'm hallucinating and she's not really here. Tell me this is just a bad dream.

As my stiff legs loosened up enough to walk over to the two of them, it seemed like every customer in the place was staring at me and laughing.

I'll show 'em. I can stand up for myself.

"Mom, what are you doing here? My shift isn't over till eleven, and I have my own car to drive home in." I tried to sound confident.

"You're not working here anymore," she said, showing me who was still boss. "I've explained our situation to Mr. Tucci, and he understands that it was a mistake to hire you. So get your things and come home right now," she ordered, starting out the door without waiting for a rebuttal.

God, can I please evaporate right now? Make me invisible because I can't bear to be here—embarrassed and ashamed. Please give me the courage to drive far away from that house and not go back.

Little had changed from the schoolhouse by the lake.

My mother was living in a situation she couldn't control. Dad still drank a lot of gin in his back room off the garage. Afraid she'd see someone she knew, she rejected the help that recovery meetings might have given her. Instead, she turned her attention to me, her vulnerable teenage daughter whom she felt she could control. I was very much under her thumb, and the only job she considered suitable for me was to be a babysitter.

So I caved, as I would over and over again, and started the search for a summer babysitting job.

I didn't have to look far. An acquaintance of my mother had a friend on Cape Cod with two little children who needed an au pair for the summer.

Mother helped me pack and drove me to work for Patty Smith and her family.

THE OUTSIDER

The first thing I noticed about Patty were her skinny calves. I had always wanted to be five inches taller with longer legs— more inches to accommodate more calories. The second thing I noticed were her two small children clinging to her skinny calves, one on the left and one on the right, like they feared they were about to be eaten by a hungry bear.

Oh, brother! How beautiful, brilliant, and charming do I have to be to seduce those two kids away from their mother?

Patty blamed the kids' reluctance with me on first day jitters and showed me to my room, where I unpacked and silently prayed that her children would warm up to me soon. I showered and went downstairs to try and break the ice with the children. Patty and her husband were going out for the evening, so she familiarized me with the kitchen and told me what to make for dinner.

From the beginning, things did not go well. As instructed, I fixed black beans and rice for their dinner.

After one bite the boy announced, "I'm not hungry. I like beans the way Mommy makes them."

"I'm not hungry either," the girl said. "Can I go play in the playroom?"

"Well, you two, you're going to be hungry later. Do you want something else? Maybe some scrambled eggs and toast?"

"No!" they shouted in unison.

I was trying hard. Though not a parent, I knew that if they didn't eat any dinner, they'd be needling their parents to feed them later. Patty and her husband would come home, tired and maybe a little drunk. The last thing they needed to greet them were two hungry kids demanding a meal. If I were good at my job, that would be taken care of. They'd be sound asleep with full bellies, and Mom and Dad could go play around. My job was to keep the kids out of their hair.

The children were resolute and refused to eat. Defeated on the dinner front, I watched cartoons with them until their eight o'clock bedtime.

After the kids changed into their pajamas, the boy announced, "I don't want to go to bed now. Mommy lets us stay up later on Fridays."

"That's not what she told me. Bedtime is eight o'clock sharp." Then, softening my tone and smiling, I tried something else. "Come on, pick out a story and I'll read it to you. I can even act it out."

I was relieved to see the little girl start to pick one out for me to read. But then, glancing at her brother, she changed her tune. He was determined to be difficult. She took her lead from him.

"I don't want you to read to me. I want my Mommy! Go away!" She sobbed as if she were genuinely under attack.

"C'mon." I sighed in defeat and swept the bangs out of her teary eyes. "Let me tuck you into your bed. Mommy will be home soon."

I closed the doors to both of their rooms and went to mine. I hoped they'd quickly go to sleep.

For the next few days, we tried enticing the kids with the neighborhood pool. We sent them to day camp one morning and left them with Grandma other mornings. Nothing worked. And all the distraction shouldn't have been necessary if I were successfully taking charge of those children. The same awkward scenario played itself out until Patty felt she had no recourse but to let me go.

"The chemistry wasn't good. There was nothing more we could do," she admitted apologetically. "It just wasn't working."

No, it wasn't working, I repeated, packing and tearfully waiting for Mom to pick me up, internalizing every rejection I'd received that week as though it were a life sentence to failure. I had no one then to tell me that I was really okay, that no one could have handled those spoiled children.

After getting out of her car, Mom faced Patty with apologies.

"Patty, I'm so sorry it didn't work out. Marilea has little experience with babysitting," she said, glaring at me.

The children were hiding in a closet, but I faced Patty solemnly before getting in the car.

"I'm so sorry, Patty. Wish it could have worked out differently. Sure hope you can find a replacement soon."

"Oh, don't worry. We will." She waved as we drove away.

I got the feeling she'd been there before with other hapless girls. But I still felt awful. My mother did nothing to counter those self-defeating feelings.

The silence weighed heavily on me as she drove home, so I turned on the radio. Mother appeared to be furious with me. Once again I had embarrassed and disappointed her. Glancing sideways, I recognized the familiar set of her jaw, heard the manipulative sighs, watched her moist hands gripping the steering wheel.

Reassurance was what I needed, some words of comfort to take the sting out of the experience. But she withdrew from me on that long ride back to the house, and I was frightened. Without an ally in my family, I felt completely alone.

From that day forward I decided to double down on my attempts to measure up to my mother's expectations. She was sad herself much of the time, and I often blamed myself. I felt I needed to right things with her and do what she wanted. Lost in the shuffle somewhere, I was unable to assert my independence, certain that if I didn't have Mother's approval, I would have no one.

DEB

My mother's life was way too heavy for me.
—Sue Monk Kidd[7]

After we moved, my mother escalated her social climbing, and she wanted me to go to private school. But, for one of the few times I can remember, I stood up to her: I insisted on remaining in public school.

"Marilea, it's a privilege to be able to go to private school. Won't you try to see it that way and not as a form of punishment?"

"It is a form of punishment to pull me away from my only two friends in this town and start over. I want to stay in school here."

Then came the pursed lips and the heavy sigh of frustration as she left the kitchen.

I felt gnawing anxiety the few times I was honest and asserted myself with my mother. Even when we weren't butting heads, I was still running to the refrigerator and slathering Miracle Whip on leftover chicken in the middle of the night. My self-hatred had become a deep and festering wound by the time I was a teenager.

When I was eight years old and lonely in my house, I ate for comfort. When I was ten and ostracized at school, food continued to soothe me. In eighth grade when kids started a rumor about me, overeating again served to numb the pain for a little while.

My food addiction remained the same. It was the playing field, the triggers, that changed.

That fall before going off to Wheaton College, Mom got her way on one thing. I was presented to Boston society. Preston was my escort, the one thing that made the evening bearable. Maybe she thought that becoming a debutante was a form of insurance, a way to guarantee that I'd follow a certain path in life: upwardly mobile, Ivy League, rich.

I hated posturing like that in my long satin gown. I'd started putting on weight, and my upper arms were flabby. I felt like such a puppet, living out my mother's dreams for her.

My dad didn't appear to be comfortable either. But he adored my mother and, despite his drinking, tried in many ways to give her what she wanted.

She ran the store.

BAGGAGE

I took the train to Princeton as often as I could my first year at Wheaton. Preston and I went to all the football games that fall but spent much of our time exploring each other. Our lovemaking was the way I remember eating an avocado for the first time: surprisingly delicious and mellow. I couldn't get enough of him, and I was so happy, really happy, for the first time in my life.

So engrossed in being in love, we wrote reams of letters back and forth, yet Preston managed to keep up his grades. I had to drop Organic Chemistry, unarguably one of the hardest courses in any college. That double F for two semesters ruined my GPA, and I barely graduated three years later.

We were sometimes careless when we made love, and by early spring I had a pregnancy scare. My period was late, and, feeling frightened, I called him, certain I could trust him.

A week later, my knight in shining armor dropped me like a virus. It was over spring break, and we were coming home from a date. He'd been acting chilly all evening, but I never saw it coming.

Pulling into my driveway, he turned off the engine and turned to look at me.

"Marilea, we need to break up. We're getting too serious."

He didn't offer to hold my hand. He didn't sound or look sorrowful at all.

I wasn't registering any of it yet—that I had lost him. *This wasn't really happening. It's just a bad dream.*

"Did you hear me, Marilea?"

"But Preston, it was just that once. I'll be more careful from now on and go on the pill," I promised, scrambling to keep him.

"I'm sorry. We need to stop now before it gets any more serious. We're lucky nothing happened." He sounded relieved that we hadn't gotten into trouble, not sad that we were breaking up.

That's all. Just relief. To be rid of me.

I stared at him.

"I've got plans," he went on, trying to fill in the empty space between us. "I want to go to medical school. I can't get too serious about anyone right now."

I already am serious. I want to marry you and be a doctor's wife. Like day into night, my world grew dark. I was screaming, but no sound came out of my mouth.

Growing impatient with me, he turned on the ignition to leave, and I felt my heart leap into my throat. "We can't see each other anymore, Marilea. I'm sorry."

Just like that? Am I so easy to walk away from? I felt as though the wolf had just blown my stick house down.

I grasped for the ring Preston had given me in January for my birthday, a garnet, my birthstone, engraved with "Love, Preston." I never took it off my finger.

"Keep it," he said, glancing at my left hand.

I felt like a worthless cow, but greedy, too, for wanting to keep it.

Speechless, I got out of his car and went into my house, blurry-eyed.

Before going up to bed, I opened the refrigerator and ate all of the leftover apple pie with a half a quart of vanilla ice cream.

I had long since lost the attention of my brother, my father was slipping away more and more into the bottle, and now Preston was gone. I retreated further into that empty space where young girls live—young girls who don't know how to love themselves.

DOÑA TINI

I found myself sauntering past their favorite shady spot, hungry for just that kind of attention.

"De quien tú eres, Maria?"

Those impudent words wafted through the air from the same group of men leering at me and sitting in the shade at the end of every day. They had finished their jobs and were listless with nothing more to do. Not in a hurry to get home to the same boring wife and screaming kids, they probably felt that catcalling the new gringa was a hospitable thing to do. A two-hundred-pound, nineteen-year-old college girl, I ate it up, secretly wondering which one of them I would favor in the bushes.

I was doing volunteer work at San Sebastián Christian Service Center deep in the rain forest of Puerto Rico. It was about as far away from New England as you could get, and that pleased me since I was too fat to be attractive to anyone back in the States. At school the previous spring, I took a job at the snack bar at Wheaton to gorge for free on tuna fish and pizza as I continued to indulge my food addiction. After Preston dumped me, my eating was off the charts.

My parents saw that I needed a distraction; volunteer work had given me a sense of purpose, and, when helping others, I usually felt better about myself for a time. So they found a mission in need of English-speaking volunteers to do a number of tasks, including teaching English to the farmers living there. And in the Caribbean, having lots of meat on your bones was considered desirable and attractive. After my breakup with Preston, I welcomed the attention.

The first thing I noticed were the roosters trumpeting every morning—every single morning. There were no highways nearby, no car noises or large trucks downshifting. I was deep in a green and perpetually humid forest in rural Puerto Rico, where life had its own sounds and rhythms, quite apart from the rest of the island. Even in my childhood in rural Massachusetts, there was never such a feeling of separation from the world. Who needs an alarm? The noises in the countryside are more reliable.

There were several volunteers from the United States living in a dormitory, and it was a comfortable arrangement. But I never quite fit in or made friends with any of the young people there. Finding myself alone much of the time, I met Doña Tini on one of my walks around the mission.

With a thin, wiry body that was no surprise with all the exercise she got walking up and down the nearby hills, she lived in a tiny house by herself. Her husband had died, and their two sons lived in the west coast town of Mayagüez. There was little work at the mission, and for years more and more boys had migrated to the cities to find work. Doña Tini had no daughter, so she was quite alone.

Approaching me on the footpath, she offered me her hand.

"Hello, there. I'm Teresa Lopez. What's your name?"

Returning her handshake, I answered, "Oh, you can call me Maria. I'm a volunteer at the mission."

"Maria, the volunteers usually stay close to the mission. It's easy to get lost around here. But it's good you decided to take a walk. You look thirsty. Would you like to see my little house over there?" She pointed to a small cabin surrounded by a beautiful flower garden. "I just made some fresh orange juice."

"Yes, thank you." *What a nice woman*, I marveled. *I don't feel so alone here anymore.*

She must have sensed that I needed a friend.

When not doing my chores at the mission, I spent a lot of time with Doña Tini. We spent hours talking about her life when she was a young girl. She came from a well-to-do family in Aquadilla, on the northern coast of Puerto Rico, and had run away with the gardener's son forty-five years before. Her family disowned her, but she loved her husband and never regretted her decision. They spent their lives near the mission, where her husband worked at odd jobs to support her and their two boys.

I identified with Tini: her comfortable background, her romanticism, her wild rebellion, and her loneliness.

Tortoiseshell clips held up her salt-and-pepper hair beautifully. I imagined her primping in front of the only looking glass in her place, the veins popping out of her hands and forearms like a sculptor's. *Aquí me dejaste, Luis*, she mildly chided her husband—as if the love of her life were standing beside her in the mirror, incandescent—for dying too soon and leaving her to manage on her own. *Me haces falta, amor mío, pero estoy bien*, she concluded in her daily conversation with him, reassuring him that she was fine.

She could see from my appearance and the way I inhaled food—always looking for seconds—that it was fulfilling a need in me that should have been satisfied elsewhere.

"Niña," she said, taking my hands in her own, "you're not always hungry when you eat. There's a sadness in you I also felt when I was your age. But eating so much will not make it go away."

And that was an extraordinary insight coming from a woman living in Puerto Rico, the land where *mucha carne* was the barometer of female desirability.

I barely knew her, but, strangely, I trusted her. More than that, I needed her; there was no emotional baggage between us.

My mother was embarrassed by my out-of-control weight gain, and she shamed me often, pressuring me to see a diet doctor. I felt ashamed and defensive around my family.

Sensing a door opening inside of me, a vulnerable spot, I allowed myself to consider behaving differently. I'd been there before, in France, when Madame accepted me in spite of my weakness, and while I was there, the compulsion to overeat had left me.

"Would you like to try not eating so much to see what happens? I won't promise any miracles, but if you stop hiding from your feelings, maybe in time you'll be able to understand what's really bothering you."

I said nothing, but she saw the look of hope in my eyes and felt me embracing her in agreement. From then on, she took me under her wing, just as my fifth-grade teacher, Irma Jackson, had done when I was ten, and for similar reasons. Both of those women were like heavenly angels floating around in space, landing on my shoulder when I needed them.

Never doubt the existence of angels on earth. They are everywhere.

Waking up in the morning, I eagerly anticipated the hike up to her house. She fed me a healthy breakfast, and, later, in the dormitory, I started to make healthier food choices.

Sometimes in the morning or early evening, we took short hikes around the hills behind her house. It was still cool at nine o'clock in the morning, though the dew burned off quickly when the sun rose over the hills and peeked through the trees.

"Maria, let's take a walk over to the crest of that hill," she suggested, pointing to an area that must have been at least two miles from her house.

"Will we get back before noon?" I asked, half hoping she'd scrap the idea because it was too far. I disliked heavy exercise and had the flabby thighs to prove it.

"Oh, sure. We'll walk quickly and fill our bags with fruit. I want to take some to another neighbor down near the mission. She can't walk anymore, so I'm her legs sometimes."

"Okay, but the Perez boys will be waiting for my lesson at one o'clock. I don't want to miss them."

"Don't worry. We'll be back in time." She winked as she put four empty bags in my hands.

So that was her plan: hike over to that hill and on our return fill up the bags with fruit to give to her friend. I was going to be a packhorse, and I would sweat more. Back in the States, walkers fill backpacks with weights and wear them on their backs for the same reason: to burn more calories.

When I complained of being hungry, she told me to eat an orange. The oranges were so plentiful and overripe in the summer that they were falling off the trees by the bushel. I picked one up, bit hard into the end, spit it out, and squeezed all the succulent juice into my mouth. Those oranges were the best and the sweetest, with thin rinds, and as big as small grapefruits. And there were mangoes, also falling off the trees, lying around, waiting to be eaten by swarms of hungry insects.

BEACHES

At some point later that summer, growing impatient with my weight loss, I decided to get away from the mission for a couple of days. I had a crazy notion that I would appear thinner with a tanned body. But it wasn't so easy to find a dry and sunny spot near the mission in the rain forest. Determined to get a tan and look svelte, I asked around and learned about a tiny sun belt on the southwest side of the island.

Doña Tini wouldn't approve of such an idea. So—sneaky, sneaky—I took advantage of her not being there while she was visiting her sons.

One Friday afternoon I took a cab west to Mayagüez, and then the cabbie swung back around southeast on the coastal road to a little seaside village called La Parguera, part of Lajas.

The continental shelf that wraps around Puerto Rico's southern coast is closest to shore at La Parguera. Its coral reefs are considered the finest and best ones off the island. There, along with a few other places on the island, a remarkable nighttime phenomenon occurs: a phosphorescent bay. When the waters are disturbed, they glow with millions of microscopic organisms that sparkle and create a spectacular light show. It occurs only in tropical areas, typically in mangrove-protected bays. The area was billed as a "Caribbean Dream."

The driver dropped me off in the middle of town. There were only a few buildings, and one of them was a little rooming house with two vacant rooms for tourists. Doña Amada ran the place, and she was warm and welcoming. She must have picked up her English from tourists over the years.

"What the heck are you doing here in the middle of nowhere?"

"I just wanted to get some sun for a couple of days."

She looked surprised. "But there are no beaches here."

"Yes, but it's always sunny. *Nunca llueve.*"

"Why don't you get my son to take you over to the mangrove swamp?" she suggested, pointing to a bunch of wood sticking out of the blue ocean not too far from the shore. *"Por otro lado puedes tomar sol,"* she said as she gave my hefty round body the once-over and saw why I wanted to sunbathe by myself.

"Okay, can he take me out there tomorrow morning?"

"Sure, *te va a cobrar cinco dólares.*" I would have paid anything for a chance to lie down somewhere and get the tan I thought would change my looks.

Well, I should have remembered my English skin. Once, when I was a child at the lake, I fell asleep on my stomach and came home with a back full of blisters. And New England sun isn't nearly as strong as Caribbean sun.

When Doña Amada's son came back to get me at five o'clock, I looked like a ripe tomato and, like a ripe tomato, was extremely soft to the touch.

Lord, I was in so much pain. Walking like my splayed legs had been spray-starched, all I could do was hobble around and collapse on my bed. Doña Amada was so horrified at the sight of me that she insisted on doing what she could to alleviate my pain and make me mobile so that she could pour me into a cab as soon as possible and send me back to wherever I came from.

That evening and the whole next day, I lay on my bed like a beached whale while she took care of me. For once I didn't even want to eat; there was too much pain. She put together a poultice and slathered it all over my body, first on the front and then on my back. It melted right into my burning flesh while I dozed on and off all day, and then she put on more. I don't know what the ingredients were, but it worked miracles. It probably had the Puerto Rican version of coca leaves in it because I was feeling no pain.

The next morning, prying my burned lips open just far enough to drink some freshly squeezed orange juice, I was feeling better and able to slither off the bed. Walking was still tricky, trying to keep my thighs from rubbing together, but I was mobile. Doña Amada could check off the first two things on her list. She just had to call a cab.

As I stood in front of the rooming house early Monday morning in a tent dress waiting for my taxi, she came out to say goodbye. In her hands was a parting gift, a big jar of her miracle poultice that I was to put on every day for a week.

"*Adiós, Maria, cuídate!*"

I thanked her, lightly hugged her, and took off in the cab, a cloud of dust trailing behind us.

JETTY

Doña Tini was delayed by illness in Mayagüez and didn't get back to the mission before I left with the other volunteers. I missed saying goodbye to her but somehow knew I would see her again.

Stopping in San Juan for a few days before I left the island, I almost died—and horribly at that. Swimming out in the surf, I got caught in a current in front of one of the jetties that protruded from the beach. The breaking waves were pushing me closer and closer to it, and I wasn't strong enough to swim out of the way. As I came close to being bashed to death, it looked like my time on earth would soon be over. And in that moment, I let go of my hold on life, or maybe, once again, my desire for it. I stopped struggling and prepared to die, not crying or screaming for help, just accepting that it was my time.

You would have had to feel the hydraulic power of the huge waves pushing me closer to those sharp rocks to understand why I gave up so easily. The peace that filled me then was a gift—a respite from everything in my life.

That transformative moment ended abruptly. I awoke from my reverie to the sound of splashing water and yelling all around me.

"*Miren! Ahí está!* Go 'round in front of her!" I heard them shouting with varying degrees of hysteria. That brought me to my senses, and I shouted out, *"Aquí estoy!* I'm over here! Help me!"

Suddenly, I was being rescued by four tall, tanned, and Hollywood-gorgeous lifeguards. As they carried me to shore, I imagined I had died and gone to heaven. But no, I just got lucky that those young men were doing their job so well.

And all four of them were necessary to lift me up and carry me back to the beach.

THE PRINTER

Hell is empty and all the devils are here.

—William Shakespeare[8]

It was spring vacation my sophomore year at Wheaton when all the hip college kids were going to Florida and flaunting their beautiful bodies in bikinis.

Not yet ready to put on a bathing suit, I continued to hide in muumuus, too ashamed to bare my flabby thighs. Flying to Bermuda alone, I stayed in a hotel room alone until a couple of girls invited me to hang out with them. A picture I took showed Mom and Dad I could make friends and have fun.

At a nearby bar I met a local named Samuel. He bought me a coke and invited me back to his smelly printer's shop where he made a block of my name. Then we took a ride to the beach on his motorcycle but ended up at his hut in the woods. I could hear the waves crashing, his sweat covering me like oil. Not protesting was the only way I knew how to get male attention.

When we were done, we went outside. He lit a cigarette and then spat out in a voice as hard as a brick, "You know, I could have killed you here tonight."

I froze, at the same time grateful that maybe he took pity on me because I was fat. There was a thin smile on his face after he took one more drag and tossed the cigarette into the woods.

Samuel turned, got on his motorcycle, and drove away, leaving me to walk back to the hotel. I was twenty, and I've never forgotten his words.

Those shattering words and all the other bullets I've dodged in my life.

BANANAS

The following summer I did go back to the mission to volunteer as an English teacher. Many of the same volunteers were there from the previous summer. But I was different. I wasn't as heavy and felt more confident about my appearance.

Doña Tini had gotten ill with cancer during the past year and had to move to Mayagüez to live with one of her sons. I went there to visit her when I could.

I was enjoying her company at lunch soon after I'd arrived. "How are you, Maria? You look wonderful."

"I'm okay, Doña Tini. It's been a difficult year at school. I miss my boyfriend so much. I really loved him."

"Yes, I know, niña. But open your heart—you will love again."

Well, I did open my heart and fell in love (at least I thought so) with Angelo, a handsome, passionate, angry orphan adopted by a mission family to bring in money through his labor. He was a sugar-cane cutter and, love or not, we fell head over heels in lust.

Spending many weekends with him and his family, away from the dorm, I learned to love the combination of bacalao and platanos. If I had been a Puerto Rican girl, I wonder if this arrangement would have been so easily tolerated. But since gringas had a reputation for being loose and immoral, everyone at the mission looked the other way. Doña Tini had allowed love to rule

MARILEA C. RABASA

her when she was my age, and she supported me all the way. She told me later in a letter that she hoped I would marry Angelo and stay in Puerto Rico. I had become, she often told me, the granddaughter she had always wanted.

Those two summers were life-changing experiences for me. I acquired the teaching bug, learned to speak Spanish fluently, and became comfortable in Hispanic culture.

My parents were worried I would run off and marry a Puerto Rican, which almost happened, so they flew down at the end of the summer and brought me back with them just to be sure.

As soon as I saw them, my bubble broke. My fantasy world, my rebellion, would have to end, and I mercilessly broke up with Angelo. He shrugged and mumbled, *"N'importa.* You gringas are all alike." Then he turned and whacked me across the face, knocking me down.

WASP

Back in the States, I continued to think about Preston and tried to get over him by falling under the spell of an interesting assortment of men. In the spring of my junior year, I met a black student named Jonas at a Harvard Law School mixer. All the months we dated, I kept him a secret from my mother and father.

"Marilea, it's easier if you do it for me while my head's on your lap," he advised, as I prepared the same routine with tweezers that I had done before. "I can't get to the roots myself."

"Okay, lean your head to the side so I can get a better angle."

Only a woman deeply in love would spend hours with a man gently digging the ingrown hairs out of his facial beard, carefully absorbing the oozing blood in a Kleenex. He was a strikingly handsome man.

Jonas graduated from the law school the following year, and just before he left Cambridge, he asked me to marry him and move to Jackson, Mississippi.

On our last phone call, I was standing in the kitchen while my mother was peeling potatoes over the sink.

"Make up your mind, Marilea," he said, growing impatient with me. "I love you, and I want to spend the rest of my life with you. Please, come away with me."

Glancing at my mother on the other side of the room, choking on my need to please her and unable to follow my heart, I muffled my answer to him on the phone so that Mother couldn't hear me.

"Jonas, I'm so sorry. I can't marry you." I disconnected—and climbed ever more deeply into my mother's web.

CLOSED WINDOWS

After graduating from college, I lived with my parents in Massachusetts, officially a grown-up but not ready to grow up and leave the nest. I had a degree in French and Spanish and was certified to teach, so I subbed in my old high school.

For nine months I lingered there, trying to figure out what to do with the rest of my life. I read Nietzsche and Sartre, listened to Rachmaninoff, wrote sappy poems, and shivered in the cold silence between my parents.

I binged on food often and purged in the downstairs powder room after my parents had gone to bed. Taking a sponge to wipe off the wall and toilet, I should have also opened the window.

Walking by in the morning, I could smell the strong odor.

Mother never said a word about it.

DINNER HOUR

"Sid, your dinner's getting cold!" Mother shouted from the back hall to the garage, not bothering to conceal her frustration. "I called you ten minutes ago."

"Marilea," she asked, returning to the kitchen, "would you get the margarine out of the fridge?"

She stood in front of his chair with a knife in her hand, slicing the corn off the cob that I had just placed, steaming, on Dad's plate. I watched this operation every time we had fresh corn in the summer. Dad had dentures and couldn't use his teeth to tear the juicy kernels off the cob.

Twenty-two and still living at home, I was the buffer my parents needed to remain civil at meal times—a distraction, someone else to worry about so they didn't have to focus on each other.

Dad came from his back room into the kitchen, swaying slightly, having enjoyed a solo cocktail hour with his Gilbey's. His face was flushed, his hair all mussed. He was only sixty, but he looked a decade older.

"Thank you for dinner, dear." Facing my mother across the table, trying to be compliant, he knew he was doing the two things that infuriated her most: smoking and drinking.

Dad looked at her with shame and great love, as well as gratitude that she was still around to cut the corn off the cob.

She was seething with anger. He was reeking with cigarette smoke and gin. I was a reluctant witness to the sad, quiet tragedy of two ill-suited people, still married, facing old age together.

"Can I clean up the kitchen?" I offered, looking for where she left the knife.

HARVARD MEN

I needed to get away from my parents to test my wings, though I was still under theirs. My mother suggested looking for a job at Harvard, and it didn't occur to me to look elsewhere. Applying for an entry-level position in the history department, I got the job. Then, deciding to move into Boston with a friend in need of a roommate, I was at last on my own.

That branch of the history department was housed back then in an old brick building between Harvard Square and Central Square. I was hired as the receptionist, the first person you see when you come into the building, so it was important to look good.

It was a heady, stimulating place to work. Henry Kissinger held a powerful position in Washington at the time, and a few of his friends and academic cronies worked in that building. Most of them were pure academics and avoided the limelight. But they wrote books and articles that defined much of what was going on both in our government and in post–World War II Europe.

Mom and Dad were thrilled that I was working at Harvard, my father's alma mater. They wished I'd meet a Harvard man, get married, and live happily ever after. They didn't know about Jonas. They hoped I'd gotten my "foreign men are sexy" rebellion out of my system in Puerto Rico, but I had not. A year and a half after I started my job, Angel M. Rabasa walked into my building to meet with another historian, and that was the beginning of the turbulent relationship that changed my life.

My new boyfriend was a Cuban American graduate student at Harvard, and he was there on a teaching fellowship. Angel was charming, intelligent, and had ambition. My parents warmed to him right away.

They were grateful for someone suitable to take their twenty-five-year-old daughter off their hands.

THE 5:35

L ike clockwork, my unexpressed feelings built up during the week, and by Saturday I exploded.

Scarfing down a distressing amount of junk food, I held a heavy missile inside.

I waited for my roommate to go out, and then I drank a lot of hot liquids and stuck my finger down my throat till the watery food came back up all over the toilet, floor, and the opposite wall. I had a lot of cleaning to do to cover my tracks. Air freshener wasn't enough, and there was no window to open.

Just like Mom, though, my roommate never said a word about what I was doing.

Those overeating spells, like a reliable train catching the work crowd at Grand Central, arrived weekly and for many years.

My teeth were a mess. Disintegrating inside my mouth like melting mints, many of them were drilled, root-canaled, and crowned. Collateral damage.

I enjoyed laughing gas only once, but my mouth was nothing to laugh about. I was so poor that I had the work done at Boston University Dental School.

"What can I expect for my teeth from now on?" I asked one of the students.

"Your teeth will need constant reparative work for the rest of your life."

Consequences were starting to mount, but they were not enough to stop me.

BROKEN PIECES

A ngel had a lot of charisma, a quality that would serve him well later on. He literally swept me off my feet, and that's when I should have known I was in trouble. When the pants came off, the blinders went on. And I was in love again.

Only four months into our relationship, however, Angel left me on my own, as he had to go to Bogotá, Colombia, to write his PhD thesis.

At work, my perennially smiling supervisor, Ellie, decided that two years was enough to put up with me and my slinky dresses. Appearing to be magnanimous, she couched the letdown in this way:

"Marilea, you are capable of doing so much more! You're wasting your abilities here!" *Go now and sin no more, Mary Magdalene. Shape up and get a life.*

So, I got fired and took an unexpected turn down a new path: I decided to go to art school. Though I loved going to museums and seeing the works of all the great artists, I'd never done any artwork of my own. Nevertheless, I entered a two-year program in interior design at a local college—and was determined to complete it in one year.

Perfectionism 101.

Make My Parents Proud of Me.

Subletting Angel's studio while he was away served a new purpose. Something had snapped inside my head, and I found myself descending into a dark cave of isolation where I limited human contact except when it was absolutely necessary.

Without Angel, I was a mess.

A few years earlier my mother, appalled by my appearance, had taken me to a diet doctor to lose weight. He introduced me to diet pills—amphetamines. I really liked taking them, not so much to reduce my appetite as to elevate my mood. I used them on and off, and they were easy to get from a doctor. Diet mills seemed to be on every block back then. But at this time they really helped me deal with the pressure of school. So I found a mill near me and got some more.

Taking a two-year course load in one year to finish quickly, I put myself under a lot of pressure. Popping handfuls of amphetamines to stay awake to do all my drawings, I spent hours at my drafting board and routinely got four hours of sleep at night.

As I raced toward a state of complete exhaustion, I felt the need to take more control of my life. The bulimia stopped in its tracks, and my engine went into reverse: I actually feared food for the first time.

Take control of my life . . . Anorexia nervosa, for some women, is about trying to maintain a sense of control. I suffered from this other eating disorder, disruptive and dangerous, soon after I'd started art school.

A typical day went like this:

I got up at 6:00 a.m. sharp and had a cup of black coffee. Breakfast was exactly one-half cup of cooked Wheatena. I savored it slowly, teeny bites at a time, while I watched the early news. Lunch was exactly two of the rectangular Venus wheat crackers that aren't in the store anymore. After all these years, the flavor is still on my tongue. With the crackers I had exactly one cup of diluted Campbell's tomato soup. Then dinner was the same as lunch, at 6:00 p.m. sharp.

"Exactly."

"Sharp."

When my classes started in June and lunch was at school, I ate a cup of plain yogurt instead of soup and crackers.

For six months, except for going back and forth to school, I kept to myself and kept up the diet and ritual. Finally, though, I couldn't stand the hunger.

Body wisdom is smart; I was starving and it knew it. Food was always on my mind. Before, in the midst of a food binge, I'd felt weak and self-indulgent, loathing myself. When I restricted food intake, I admired myself. My whole life had become a wrestling match—a love-hate battle with my self-esteem—using food as the arbiter.

Predictably the lack of sleep and food pushed me right to the edge of a cliff. Complete with paranoia and hallucinations, I had a nervous breakdown.

Cowering in Angel's studio, I listened to the footsteps on the floor above me, too afraid to sleep but more afraid to be awake. *Oh my God, I can hear the footsteps above me. What can I do?*

I put a chair under the doorknob, certain that someone was going to break in and kill me. When my windows filled with light, I felt safer. But as soon as the sun went down, my fear came back as I hid inside the studio.

Mom and Dad had been distracted by their own problems throughout much of my childhood, but seeing me then, thirteen years after I had chosen the wrong vein in the hopes of ending my life, ninety pounds and hollow-eyed, even they couldn't ignore the serious psychological problems threatening me.

At first my father was quick to blame the social unrest going on in the country.

"It's what's going on with all those young people on campuses. That's what's got her going nuts," he said, shaking his head.

So began two years of intensive therapy they secured for me with Dr. K., a well-respected psychiatrist in Cambridge. Twice a week I drove my Volkswagen over to his office for my fifty-minute appointments. And for the first week or so, I didn't speak. Curling myself into a fetal position, I lay on his nice plush carpet and sobbed.

The fact that I agreed to see him was a good sign; I still had hope. The waterways on this magical mystery tour were my tears, my will to live, my flotation. And Dr. K. was my gentle guide as my dark world grew lighter.

His patience disarmed me. He had no expectations. And I wasn't desperate for his approval.

The complete lack of script between us enabled me to start trusting him, and that's when I began talking about the sources of sadness in my life.

We discussed how suicide might solve my problems. How I felt like the black sheep of the family, a burden and an embarrassment. The complete alienation I felt from my siblings, how I was terrified to do anything to piss my mother off. At the same time I wanted to be free of her and be my own person. But I didn't have a clue who that was—not one damn clue.

If they told me I was smart, I believed them. If they told me I was dumb, I believed them—I was as hollow as an eggshell and just as fragile.

Dr. K. listened patiently as I went on and on about people without faces plotting to kill me, voices without sound—fears, like a child's, that only surfaced in the night. At some point in therapy, my hallucinations began to fade the way scenes in a movie some-times peter out during the credits. But not before I went to see my college advisor with the intention of dropping out of art school.

Mr. Jones nodded with the familiarity of having heard this before when I tearfully told him I was going out of my mind.

"I'm hearing voices at night, and I'm sure they're coming to get me."

"Who's coming to get you?" He sounded like he believed me.

"I don't know, I'm just afraid all the time!" I was wide-eyed and sobbing, frightened by my behavior.

"Marilea, go home. It's November. Take a long holiday and then come back to finish the year in January. You're exhausted and need to stop working and rest."

His advice sounded comforting; I threw out the amphet-amines for good and started eating like before.

I got back on the 5:35.

AWAY

A ngel and I had kept up our correspondence while he was in Bogotá. But like so much of what defined me then and for most of my life, I covered up habits that brought me shame, fearing the same criticism and judgment my mother had often heaped on me.

He knew art school was going well and that I had been in therapy since he left. But he knew nothing about my use of amphetamines, the eating disorders, or my nervous breakdown. I was afraid to show him my dark side.

My therapy with Dr. K. had been continuing uninterrupted. Gradually I felt relieved of the crippling paralysis that had been holding me back, and my depression lifted somewhat, though never entirely. I was still secretly binging and purging at regular intervals, a powerful addiction I had no interest in giving up at that point. Even with my therapist, I covered up behaviors he might have helped me address.

Soon after the New Year, Angel returned from Colombia, and it was a happy reunion.

"Angel, let's get married," I proposed over dinner a few months after he returned. "We love each other. We'll both be happier if we settle down and make a commitment to each other. We could have a wonderful life together." I reached across the table to kiss him.

"Yes, Marilea. I want to marry you," he answered, kissing me back. "I missed you, and it's so good to be back with you now."

The next day, excited about our future together, we found a secondhand jewelry shop in Harvard Square where we picked out my engagement ring: an antique with three colors of gold bands—pink, yellow, and white.

His studio where I had been living, fresh with memories of a brief but frightening period in my life, was too small for us.

"Angel, I bumped into Sally, remember her on the fourth floor? She's moving out next month to follow her boyfriend to Berkeley, and she said there would be no problem for us to pick up her lease. It's perfect for us: one bedroom, just the right size for the furniture we have."

"Sounds great, Marilea." I loved the way he trilled the r in my name. He'd lived in the United States since he was twelve, but he had a Spanish accent you could cut with a knife.

My fiancé was offered a job at a think tank in McLean, Virginia, and he accepted it. At the same time, he applied for a position in the Foreign Service at the Department of State. We would wait to hear the results that fall, but I wholeheartedly supported his plans. My life in New England had been suffocating me, and I embraced the idea of getting away. I remember the joy and anticipation of moving to the nation's capital and starting my life with that good and talented man, my mooring and anchor.

Our wedding was on a warm day in September. We both giddily toasted our parents for all they had done for us. As I looked around at my family and friends on that day, I felt happy, the sadness and emptiness pushed down, submerged, out of sight.

Dr. K. made a surprise visit on my wedding day. No one in the world knew my mind better than my dear doctor, who was instrumental in coaxing me out of my misery and helping me find the will to keep going. He knew what none of us remotely thought about on that day: that my well-being would continue to be challenged, that I was a damaged young woman and would require a lot of work to develop a healthy self-concept.

There was no time, just then, to do the work. Angel and his budding career were beckoning, and I'd better hop on that train before it took off. My emotional health would have to wait.

The day after our wedding, my husband and I packed a moving truck and moved to Alexandria, Virginia. He had a good job, but we were waiting to hear from the Foreign Service. That was his real dream: to be caught up in political intrigue and excitement around the world. Having worked around some well-connected academics at Harvard during the Nixon years, he wanted to hobnob with other powerful people on an international level. Maybe even become an ambassador.

The State Department accepted his application right away, and we were scheduled for our first posting four months later.

Managua, Nicaragua, here we come.

It could have been Siberia.

Part Two

MUDDLING THROUGH THE MIDDLE

You'll get mixed up, of course, as you already know.
You'll get mixed up with many strange birds as you go.
So be sure when you step. Step with care and great tact
and remember that Life's a Great Balancing Act.
Just never forget to be dexterous and deft.
And never mix up your right foot with your left.

—Dr. Seuss, *Oh, the Places You'll Go!*[9]

NO PRESSURE!

A beautiful wedding—a day to remember,
We'll never forget the sixth of September.
They're living in Virginia, but the Foreign Service calls.
Some distant spot may welcome them before
next year's snow falls.
We're blessed with six grandchildren,
but the day will surely come,
When the newlyweds will call and say,
"You've got another one."

—My father's Christmas poem, December 1975

VOLCANOES

As soon as they opened the passenger door on the airplane, a wall of hot air knocked me over. Having suffered through plenty of hot and humid summers, this air stunned me. *Hell, this is why they call it a "hardship post."* In the Caribbean there were ocean breezes that offered relief. It had never felt so oppressive to me, either, in the rain forest of Puerto Rico.

I thought I would faint as soon as my feet hit the pavement.

The weather, I soon discovered, would be the least of my problems. Nicaragua was becoming a political hot spot soon to explode not unlike the nearby volcanoes. In 1976, that sleepy little country in Central America entered one of the most turbulent periods in the country's history. Following Angel there, I was about to have a front-row seat for watching the unfolding of a revolution that would spread all over Central America, exacerbated in no small part by a catastrophic 1972 earthquake.

Nicaragua has nineteen active volcanoes that form a northwest-southeast running chain mostly inside the geological feature called the Nicaraguan Depression. Managua lies within an active volcanic zone known as the Central American Volcanic Chain. The city has a long history of volcanic and seismic activity that arises from the relative movements of two intersecting crustal plates near the southwestern border of Central America.

Whatever the technical cause was, the earthquake that occurred on December 23, 1972, had a magnitude of 6.2. With two powerful aftershocks in rapid succession, there were widespread casualties among Managua's residents: 6,000 were killed, 20,000 were injured, and over 250,000 were left homeless.

What was particularly striking to me as the embassy car drove us to our temporary residence was the visible destruction to the city—four years later. It was clear to me then—and would become clearer in the next two years—that the man in charge didn't care much for his own countrymen.

Like the friction between the crustal plates inside the earth, the dissension within the two parties in power, the Liberals and the Conservatives, continued to come to the surface. Opposition to the regime, which had begun well before the earthquake, increased rapidly among the lower classes and even among members of the middle and upper classes who were fed up with President Somoza's corruption.

Angel was thrilled and fascinated to be in Managua at such a pivotal time in history and made friends quickly with local politicians and journalists. He was also a magnet for danger and started cultivating relationships with a number of the Conservatives who were in opposition to Somoza, among them Pedro Joaquín Chamorro, the editor of *La Prensa* and a virulent critic of the president.

Again, fear knocked on my door. It was always close by, leaving me vulnerable.

TRAIN WRECK

We entertained often and lavishly at our home in the Ticomo section along the Carretera Sur, and though Angel was a junior officer at the time, the embassy was generous in providing all the help we needed, from gardeners to cooks and housemaids.

Under a lot of pressure to impress his superiors at the State Department, Angel was determined to succeed and move up the career ladder quickly. He was an expert at political banter and had loved sparring with the best minds around at Harvard during his years there. Never in his league intellectually, I made the mistake, once, of piping in with my two cents' worth at a reception we hosted.

"Shut up, Marilea," Angel immediately barked.

It was as if the parts of a furnace started slowing down, losing steam.

In disbelief at my husband's rude and boorish behavior, I held on to my composure and my smile. Then, looking toward the house, I broke the stunned silence with some levity.

"Did you hear that? Something just shattered on the floor inside. Gloria needs some help with the servers," I said, relieved to have found what I thought was a graceful exit.

I slunk away from that circle, but not before noticing one wife had a smug look on her face that said, "Better you than me." Hob-nobbing among the guests for the rest of the evening, hiding in the kitchen much of the time, I pretended to carry on as if nothing had happened. With a fake smile plastered from ear to ear, I thanked everyone for coming. *Oh yes, what a lovely evening.* But I was stifling a scream that wanted to get out. Instead of giving voice to my indignation, I stuffed myself with leftovers.

The next day Angel came home with a peace offering: a beautiful lapis lazuli necklace that cost more than we could afford and a trip to cool Matagalpa that weekend to get away from the heat. He knew he had crossed the line with me.

Matagalpa, known as the "Land of Eternal Spring," is a short two-hour drive north of Managua. The rise up in elevation, to 2,200 feet, provided a breathtaking view of the nearby rain forest.

We stayed in a comfortable hotel set deep in an abundance of trees and vegetation, with beautiful flowers everywhere and moss hanging from the trees. After a long walk in the forest surrounding us, we had a nice dinner and went to bed early, strangers under the covers.

My husband, with an occasional lapse in good behavior, was not the first to love a woman who did not know how to love herself. This unwelcome intruder in our marriage kept me isolated in the dark cave of perennial self-loathing. All children deserve to feel wanted and loved, and their self-love grows out of that. But when I was young, I felt unimportant and dismissed much of the time; I spent my childhood screaming voiceless for attention. No man would ever be able to give me what I'd needed nor would I be able to ask for it until I had mastered two simple words and meant them: *I am.*

The breakfast buffet in the morning was a delicious send-off from the hotel management. There were tables and tables of sumptuous dishes—*nacatamales, gallo pinto,* and fried sweet plantains. I particularly enjoyed the sweet plantains, a big difference from the plain boiled plantains I used to eat with salted codfish (bacalao) in Puerto Rico.

For a woman who used food to escape, this was heaven. Where to start? Where to stop? When the troll appeared, I just ate and ate—no limits—until the discomfort was so great that I couldn't eat anymore. Food is to a compulsive overeater what drugs are to drug addicts: temporary relief. After the first few bites, I didn't even taste the food.

We drove right home after breakfast. I was in the middle of an "episode," and on the other end of that zip wire was the need to undo the damage, to purge until my throat started bleeding. Angel and I hadn't been married long, but he must have known what I was doing. Maybe he just didn't want to confront me with my food addiction. As with my mother, the attitude seemed to be that if we didn't talk about it, then maybe it would go away. *Maybe, pfft! It won't be real if we don't acknowledge it.* Like Daddy in the back room—we could pretend some days that the gin wasn't there, and he was just a grumpy old man.

As soon as we pulled into the driveway, I ran to the kitchen and made myself a hot cup of tea. Angel drove back to the embassy to write a cable for the State Department, and Gloria had the day off. The house was empty, and I had a date with the toilet. It would be easy. No witnesses. No one to put a mirror up to my face and ask me what the hell I was doing. My dirty little secret.

I had to purge. That was the other end, so to speak, of my compulsion. If nothing else, I was damned uncomfortable with my bursting intestines, in need of relief. I also couldn't allow such overindulgence to ruin my girlish figure.

At the same time, I wanted so much to have a baby. It was what my parents expected of me. Sometimes before I purged, I looked at myself sideways in the mirror and was thrilled to see what appeared to be a pregnant belly. Only it wasn't—just a bloated one.

In the subsequent five years, I would bear three healthy children. But I have no stretch marks. My compulsion is why. My abdomen had been elasticized back and forth since I was twenty.

Hands washed. Stationed in front of the toilet with the seat up. I remember that purge like it was yesterday.

Breakfast came up easily, like big buckets of oatmeal, one after the other, with only a few thrusts of my fingers down my throat. *What a great and complete purge that one had been!*

Complete.

Like I'd gotten all of the bad stuff out all at once. *Look at me from the side! I'm as thin as a rail. I'm in control. I'm gonna hold on to it. I never need to do this again!*

Bulimics always want it to be the last time, thinking we'll be free forever of whatever we thought we were getting rid of. I was twenty-eight that year in Nicaragua, and I'm seventy-two now. There were plenty more binges in the years in between. But gradually over time the need for them trickled out and then ended. In direct proportion, perhaps, to my ability to say "*I am*" and mean it. In direct proportion to my ability to know who I was and love myself anyway.

As Angel was leaving for the embassy, I had said to him, "I'll just lie down for a while. Just need to rest. But thanks for taking me to the mountains. It was a nice break from the heat."

"Sure, baby. And I hope you know how sorry I am for being a jerk the other night," he apologized, kissing me on the mouth.

"Yeah, I know." I kissed him back, poised and ready to carry out the secret operation—the final purge—that would assure me once and for all that I was back in control of myself . . . and of my life.

I was still a child wanting to have a child. Fortunately, I still had my sanity—sort of—and a teaching degree.

THIRD WORLD

To keep busy during the day and distract myself from trying to get pregnant, I taught English and math at a nearby private school, Academia Internacional. The administrators were delighted to corral an American with teaching credentials to work at their school.

I had no résumé to offer; it was my first teaching job, and I knew nothing about teaching. But I was lucky to get some experience teaching middle school English and math to kids rich enough to pay for the privilege of getting teachers who went to college. Such was the state of affairs in public education in Nicaragua.

Taking a teaching job was a good idea, and around my twenty-ninth birthday, I became pregnant, thrilled at the thought of becoming a mother. I was determined to do everything right to ensure a healthy delivery.

Work would continue until mid-September. My due date was the twenty-fifth. On Angel's birthday, the twenty-ninth, I went into labor. Hour after endless hour, I lay on my bed in agony, without any medication, while my American neighbor came over to rub my back and try to distract me. Angel had to be at an embassy event, he argued, as though he didn't have a choice. I was furious with him but unable to give voice to my anger, quite alone in that unforgiving climate, an "elderly primipara," unschooled in child-birth and unable to bring my child into the world.

After two days, Angel could no longer ignore my screams, so he hustled me into the clinic and demanded that Dr. Mendez induce my labor. My much-awaited first child, Carter Michael, was finally born there. I was so exhausted by the time the Pitocin dilated me that I couldn't push at all. I was completely *agotada*—a wrung-out sponge.

So the nurses, before we could open our mouths to protest, put their hands on my belly to push my baby out like a football. Like . . . a . . . football! Good Lord, what if his head had gotten stuck in the birth canal, or his neck had snapped? "Oh well, so sorry, señora, there will be other babies." *In this country where women pop out babies every year and bury half of them?* I prayed for a miracle.

"*Un varoncito!*" they all exclaimed, clapping their hands, and Angel, for once in his life, was speechless. But we need not have worried: Carter was a perfect ten on the Apgar scale, a rollicking and screaming baby boy.

Once again, my guardian angel was sitting on my shoulder, protecting us from disaster.

REVOLUTION!

The politics in Managua were heating up to a dangerous level of treachery and subversion. But we couldn't have been there at a more colorful time. We got to know the Conservative opposition leader, Pedro Joaquín Chamorro, and his wife, Violeta, who would later become president of that war-torn country. Soon after Carter's birth, Angel and I took him up to Pedro Joaquín's beach house in Jiquilillo on the Pacific coast.

It was a refreshing relief to be welcomed into the Chamorros' open-air cabana with curtains flapping in the magnificent breeze and nothing but hammocks to sleep on. There was a handy servant, whom Violeta sent scurrying to the nearby market every now and then to bring us food, and plenty of ice in the cooler for drinks.

We spent a relaxing and peaceful weekend with the Chamorros. My husband represented the interests of the United States, and Pedro Joaquín chose to cultivate him in his diplomatic capacity.

I recall bold and intimate conversations. Nicaragua needed to move in another direction. The United States had been propping up the Somoza dynasty for many years, and serious political upheaval hung in the air. Three years earlier, in 1975, as if he'd had a crystal ball, Pedro Joaquín wrote in a letter to Somoza: "I am waiting, with a clear conscience, and a soul at peace, for the blow you are to deliver."

Six weeks after our visit with the Chamorros, on January 10, 1978, change did come with the assassination of our friend, brutally gunned down on his way to work at *La Prensa*. Pedro Joaquín knew exactly what might come from his many years of publicly opposing Somoza. And he knew that the time was ripe for him to take a stand.

The unrest that had been brewing steadily came to a head and erupted with Pedro Joaquín's murder. Riots filled the streets of Managua, a general strike was called, and the revolutionary soldiers prepared to do battle with President Somoza's National Guard.

My little family got out of Managua two months after Pedro Joaquín's family buried him. I was badly shaken by the growing violence all around me. The revolution began in earnest the following September, and I would feel safer just about anywhere else, terrified of staying there one minute longer than I had to.

Angel was on a roll now. He'd gotten a taste in his mouth and he wanted more: political intrigue, famous people, and excitement. It would take several years for him to get to the place he wanted to be in the Foreign Service.

But I wasn't sure what my role was in his life, other than the wife who did all the work behind the scenes and kept her mouth shut in public.

I was still so disconnected from myself.

And always afraid.

BLOOD AND WINE

We are born in innocence. . . . Corruption comes later.
The first fear is a corruption, the first reaching
for a something that defies us.

—Laura Z. Hobson[10]

Diary Entry: March–August '78: "Lived in Arlington Towers with Carter. Five completely lost and desperate months . . ."

Angel, Carter, and I were living in State Department housing in Rosslyn, Virginia. He went to work at Foggy Bottom every day, and I stayed home with my little boy. I could have reached out and made some friends there, but I was in a dark place.

Isolation was a prison I kept sentencing myself to. Avoiding other people—mirrors who might offer useful feedback—I wasn't ready to look at myself. It would take me many years to embrace that level of honesty and grow from it.

Fitting in as we moved from place to place continued to challenge me. I often, in some abstract way, felt different from those around me, a feeling I'd wished I could have overcome. Moving frequently and entering into new communities involved a skillful juggling act, and much of the time I performed well. But offstage, away from an audience, fear and self-doubt prevailed. An unrecovered food addict, one dark day I thought I'd try getting drunk.

Angel was working double time at the State Department; he was a valuable source of information on the Sandinista Revolution unfolding in Nicaragua. Instead of asking my husband to stay home more and help with our son, I stuffed my feelings.

All my emotions—happy, sad, and red-hot rage—overwhelmed me right then.

I needed numbness; I needed a drink.

Carter was down for his long afternoon nap, so I was free.

Going into our stash of wine, I grabbed a red. It didn't matter—red, white, purple—*just take the pain away, please.*

I had never been a drinker—still wasn't. But I was sick, momentarily, of food binges and rotten teeth. It was the only thing in the house that might numb me.

So I stuck the corkscrew in and turned and twisted, but I only managed to frag the cork. It broke up into tiny, irregular chunks, but the wine was still sealed in the bottle. I couldn't get it out!

I stared at that bottle of red wine. The only thing separating me from sweet oblivion was that goddamn shredded cork. How to get it out? How to free that bitter red juice so I could be liberated from my misery?

Maybe there was a better way, but all reason and logic had escaped me. Sobbing uncontrollably, I rummaged around in the kitchen drawer for an old buck knife I'd seen there.

Opening the knife, I held the wine bottle with my left hand because I was right-handed and needed some dexterity to make this work. So I stabbed at the cork, trying to push it into the bottle.

I missed.

The result was a deep gash that would require stitches. I knew this because my flesh was pulled open and stayed there as though it were held on either side by an invisible string. Even with a Band-Aid, it didn't close neatly on its own. My gaping wound was on the inside of my left thumb where the blade had pierced me instead of the cork.

Stunned by my clumsiness, I was on a mission. Bleeding profusely, I kept stabbing that cork until it finally plunged back into the bottle.

Now I could pour a drink. And then another. And then another. I drank the whole bottle like it was water and felt pretty woozy, but that's all.

Looking down at my left thumb, I went to get a Band-Aid, too embarrassed to get the necessary stitches.

I knew it would heal, eventually. It's not like it was on my nose.

GUINEA PIG

"Marilea, where is Isabel?" Angel was flying through the door and more out of breath than usual. He'd had crippling asthma all his life; it really took a toll on him, especially when he got emotional. And moving to the high altitude of Quito the previous summer had made his illness much worse.

"She took Carter to the market with her. With our trip coming up, he needs to get used to being away from me for short periods of time. When we go to Bolivia, maybe he won't miss me."

The words "miss me" rang in my ears, and I felt the panic of being separated from my toddler for the first time.

"Angel, please listen to me. I'm really uncomfortable being away from him for so long. He just got out of the hospital two months ago. It'll traumatize him. Dammit, I don't want to go away now. I just don't feel well a lot of the time."

A couple of months earlier, Carter had had an intestinal infection and was badly dehydrated, a life-threatening situation for such a young child. Four months pregnant, I held him down with the IV in his hand for two days until he recovered enough to go home. But all the antibiotics he had to take virtually destroyed his intestines along with all the good bacteria he needed to digest cow's milk. He couldn't drink it again for a long time, and my mother had to send us cases of Isomil, an awful metallic-tasting milk substitute.

It was a harrowing experience, so Angel wanted to get away for some rest and relaxation.

I agreed to accompany him on the trip because it would be an opportunity to see some of the greatest wonders in the world. But terrible misgivings about leaving Carter for two weeks kept me awake some nights.

I was picturing Isabel carrying him on her back one weekend when she'd gone to visit her family. How I must have trusted her to let her take my handsome little yellow-haired son up the mountain to visit her family for the day! Remembering what went on in today's world with child trafficking, I shuddered.

"You're the one who'll be traumatized, Marilea. He'll be fine. But please forget about that right now. We've got stuff to do. Bobby Kennedy's coming to dinner tomorrow night with Lem Billings."

"What? RFK's son? And who is Lem Billings?"

"A family friend, I think. Anyway, I met Bobby at the embassy today. He's just passing through on a trip, and I invited him to dinner."

Jeez, Angel, you'll do anything to impress State. You know how tired I've been feeling lately. What does your wife need to do this time?

"Just like that—with one day's notice? Angel, this isn't a restaurant! What am I supposed to make for dinner with so little notice?"

"Well, I asked him what he'd like, and he said, 'guinea pig.'" He grinned.

"What? Where the hell am I supposed to get a guinea pig, much less cook it?"

"Relax, Marilea, that's why we need Isabel. You need to drive her to the central market tomorrow morning and get one. She'll know what to do."

"Dammit, you always do this to me. Am I allowed to feel nervous at all? How old is Bobby anyway?"

"A little younger than we are. He graduated from Harvard a few years after I did. That's why they introduced us—we had something in common."

"Oh well, here goes nothing."

"It'll be fun, Marilea. Relax. Something to laugh about someday." Angel tried to reassure me, but I was fuming and nervous about the dinner falling short of everyone's expectations.

I wandered, then, into familiar territory. Afraid of failure or that I would embarrass Angel again, I indulged my food addiction, starting dinner before dinnertime, and then another meal after dinner—topped off by three helpings of a delicious, creamy flan I'd picked up at the store. Angel was in the mood to celebrate and decided to open a bottle of wine for dinner. I joined him with a glass or two, knowing the promise of alcohol, the numbness it provided.

Now two substances were providing oblivion: food and alcohol.

So deep in the forest, I couldn't see the trees all around me. Many years later I would recall the early years of my marriage as the time when another ominous door was starting to open.

The next morning, I drove our housekeeper, Isabel, to the open-air market in downtown Quito to get some fresh *cuy*, as they're called. She paid a few sucres to the vender and wrapped the animal in a thin towel.

"Isabel, how are we going to get a live guinea pig home with us? I don't have a cage."

"*Mire*, señora." She moved to the sidewalk and cracked its head on the pavement with one swift blow. *Whack!* That was instant, merciful death—and we'd have no problem transporting it back home. The shoppers nearby paid no attention. They'd seen the animals slaughtered before.

God, what was she going to do now? How do you cook a guinea pig?

I was glad that the kitchen was tucked away in the back of the house next to the servants' quarters. I didn't want to see how Isabel was preparing that little rodent for dinner with our guests. Watching her kill it was enough. But that was nothing to her. She grew up in a mountain village where people ate that way every day.

After Isabel had finished skinning, cleaning out, and dressing the *cuy*, she put it in a pot to marinate in the refrigerator, awaiting the spit for roasting later. Carter and I needed a nap, and we both slept for close to three hours. I was exhausted even before the evening's entertainment began.

But I needn't have been apprehensive. Angel breezed through the door at around seven o'clock with the Kennedy retinue, all of them anxious for drinks in anticipation of Bobby's dinner request. In all his South American travels, he'd neglected to indulge in that Andean treat. So, thanks to the expertise of Isabel, his wish was fulfilled that evening.

It was actually delicious, sort of like chicken but gamier. Twenty-five-year-old Robert Kennedy Jr. asked for the eye of the beast to eat and did so with great flourish. As I heard him crunching the eye between his molars, a wave of nausea came over me. But I pulled myself together as we all made appropriate noises of appreciation.

Angel had been right: it was something to remember and laugh about.

MOTHER LOVE

My son was a handful! We had one room with just mattresses so he could let off steam without breaking any bones. Sort of like a padded cell . . .

Isabel and I lay on the mattresses much of the day while he romped and wore himself out. When Angel and I weren't entertaining or being entertained in the embassy community, that is how I spent most of my days.

Isabel and her two daughters had been living with us since our arrival the previous summer, and they were a vital addition to our household. I had seen firsthand how Isabel took charge of the house and how she cared for my son. But, though I trusted her completely to manage things in my absence, I still dreaded leaving Carter for so long.

I experienced some important life passages on my own, without hands-on familial support, when I lived overseas. But Isabel—Mamá Abès, as Carter called her—as well as her two young daughters became my family while we lived in Quito. The day-to-day help, the advice on my second pregnancy: it was Isabel who was my help and comfort every day. So it wasn't difficult to entrust my little boy to her for a couple of weeks.

I just knew I'd miss him.

The plan was to fly first to Lima and then to Cuzco, where

we'd take a train down to the Urubamba Valley and then be bussed up to the vast Inca ruin of Machu Picchu. After staying at the ruins, we would return to Cuzco and catch a bus down to Puno, on the northern shores of Lake Titicaca. There we would hop onto a hydrofoil—something like a water taxi, but faster than a car. We would skim across the highest lake in the world and on the southern shore pick up a bus to La Paz. Then we would sightsee in Bolivia, fly back to Lima, and finally return to Quito. It was to be a two-week trip. An ambitious plan.

We flew to Lima as planned later in the spring.

Perhaps to salve their consciences for looting Peru and many other countries, the Spanish conquistadores built several gilded cathedrals in Lima, like the high altar of the Lima Cathedral, a magnificent sight. In 1535 Francisco Pizarro laid the first stone there, and only six years later it became his resting place.

We were both anxious to get up to Machu Picchu, so after a few days we flew to Cuzco, the old Inca capital and twelve thousand feet in the clouds. The altitude proved troublesome for Angel, but we had a comfortable hotel and enjoyed romantic dinners in front of a fire at some cozy restaurants. During the day the strong equatorial sun warmed us. But when the clouds blocked it, I understood why the sun has been worshipped as a god for centuries.

Next came the main focus of our trip, our tour of Machu Picchu. Taking a train down to the Sacred Valley along the Urubamba River to Aguas Calientes, we spent the night there before being transported up to the hidden city.

An old poster of Machu Picchu had long held a place on our living room wall, and, one of my husband's fondest wishes realized, we were finally standing there, astounded.

Angel was eager to see as much as possible in the limited

time we had, so we confined ourselves to the upper area. The Inca engineers designed the Intihuatana stone as an astronomic clock and used it as a calendar, celebrating the winter and the summer solstice, among other events. The Temple of the Sun and the Room of the Three Windows were both dedicated to Inti, the sun god.

But all the changes in altitude—from Lima at sea level, to Cuzco at twelve thousand feet, to where we were at eight thousand feet—started to bother me, no doubt because of my advanced pregnancy, and I needed to sit down while Angel kept walking. A snapshot of me sitting on the saddle of the ruin captured the saddest, weariest look on my face.

Angel decided we should catch the next bus down to Aguas Calientes, and from there we hopped on a train to Cuzco. We spent the night in a hotel there, but we hardly had time to catch our breath before we caught a bus to Puno the next day.

On a long and tiring ride in an overcrowded bus with men, children, and women in white hats, I was starting to feel sick a lot, light-headed and nauseous.

We took the hydrofoil across Lake Titicaca and boarded another overcrowded bus, this time with women in black bowlers, to La Paz. Few things impressed me after seeing Machu Picchu, and hiking around the Altiplano to see the ruins, which seemed like big vertical boulders in a desolate brown desert, didn't help my altitude sickness.

Calling home every day so Carter would hear my voice, I wish every moment spent stepping back in history had moved me, but eventually I couldn't bear being away from him and felt in my gut that something was wrong at home. After a couple of days in La Paz, we cut our trip short and flew back to Quito. Our two-week vacation in Peru and Bolivia lasted only nine days.

As I counted the moments until the taxi reached our house on the hillside facing Pichincha, memories of my labor with him, his miraculous birth, and now his beautiful pink cheeks as he romped on the grass in the morning chill filled my mind. I fantasized about our reunion just a few blocks away. Arriving with the sun at high noon, I ran to greet him as the taxi sped away.

But Carter had a blank look on his face. Far from excitedly toddling to greet me, he acted as though he didn't even recognize me.

My life has been full of lessons in love, and that was a big one. I never left my children so young again.

More bad news greeted me upon my arrival. Changing his diapers, Isabel noticed a bulge in his groin that shouldn't have been there. Perhaps that was what had been gnawing on me while I was away. Now seven months pregnant, I found myself in the kitchen enjoying Isabel's dishes at all hours. A substance user worrying about her little boy and feeling guilty for leaving him, I needed a fix. The next day Carter endured surgery for a hernia repair and another hospital stay.

Food had been the panacea to quell any uncomfortable feelings ever since I was little. It had been one of my first solutions to help me face the inevitable difficulties in life. I had no faith to draw on, spiritually bankrupt to the core.

My husband was a good man. He was ambitious and enjoyed taking risks, but he loved me and wasn't responsible for my inner turmoil. The seeds of that were planted years before he ever met me.

So we continued. I kept hoping that our fascinating life—all the busyness and hard work, the children we were blessed with— would distract me from my pain and loneliness. I'd wished I could have put it in a box and forgotten about it.

But I couldn't. It followed me.

And now it would follow me and my children.

I binged and I binged and I purged and I purged.

My baggage got heavier by the day, and inevitably, the burden fell on those closest to me.

EARTHQUAKE

The long, lazy summer drought settled onto that sleepy capital, reminding us that our electric power was hydraulic. Electricity had to be rationed, like food in a famine. For half of the day we either had or wished we had power to cook, to watch TV, or to wash our clothes. Alternatingly, the other half of Quito experienced the same inconvenience. Such was the way of life in that hardship post, but it never bothered me much. I was busy taking turns with Isabel in the padded cell with Carter.

Annalise entered the world easily between lunch and dinner, a week after my mother's birthday in August. Angel eagerly anticipated her arrival, partly because he was used to fatherhood by now, but also because he wanted a little girl. He fainted as he saw her come into the world. There I was at the other end, having just given birth, and he collapsed. Overcome with happiness, he now had the daughter he'd hoped for.

I loved my baby girl with abandon. But she had terrible colic and Isabel swaddled her right from the beginning, a common practice in many indigenous cultures. Mothers wrap their babies tightly in a cloth or swaddling band, preventing any movement of their limbs. The rationale was to totally immobilize the babies so they'd be so bored that all they could do was sleep. Many contemporary mothers might consider that a brilliant idea.

Annie fussed all the time, and I kept putting her to my breast. "Oh God, it's so sore," I muttered between feedings, "just like Carter, but at least his sister doesn't bite."

The nurse in my doctor's office gave me some nipple cream, but too soon after applying it, Annie needed to nurse again—a vicious cycle.

Oh, here it comes again: my milk is coming in, a delicious burning pressure. It's coming down and diluting the lanolin cream. Hearing her screaming, I'd think, *Okay, wipe it off now, even if it undoes the therapy it's providing.*

Here, Annie, my beautiful little girl. I don't care. I love you. Drink up.

Annie had the same congenital hernia as her brother, and at three months old she needed surgery. So we endured a fair amount of trauma that year, with another childbirth and infant and toddler surgeries.

My mother and father flew down to Ecuador toward the end of our tour to see their newest grandchild and visit the beautiful Andean country where she'd been born. They decided to come in early December and stay about a month.

On December 12 while they were in bed, a violent earthquake just off the Pacific coast shook the border between Ecuador and Colombia near the port city of Tumaco. Registering a magnitude of 8.2 on the Richter scale, it also triggered a major tsunami that caused most of the fatalities.

I was glad to be sitting high up in the Andes.

The earthquake actually left a crack in the wall of the guest bedroom where my parents had been sleeping. We would tell this story in our family for the few years afterward that my father was still alive:

Mother awoke at three in the morning and the bed was

shaking, so she shook my father. "Sid, stop shaking the bed!" she said. Then she thought, *How could he be shaking the bed like that?* It stopped and she went back to sleep.

The next morning I heard the news and told my mother about the earthquake in Colombia. At breakfast, she informed my father, "Sid, Marilea said there was an earthquake in Colombia last night."

"Oh, really? Is that why our bed was shaking, dear?" my father joked, smiling at my mother and reaching over to squeeze her arm.

Mom wrote in her Ecuador diary that their time together in Quito was happy, primarily because Dad had decided to stop drinking for the whole trip. No beer, no gin, and he lost seventeen pounds even with Isabel's great cooking. He was also, she noted with glee, easy to get along with and fun—the charmer she'd married more than forty years before.

"PSC did not have champagne on the plane—no booze for three weeks—seventeen pounds lighter. The miracle of Quito!" my mother wrote in her last diary entry.

I smile remembering that.

THREE MAIDS

When we left Quito in May of 1980, we got on the Milk Run, a series of small planes hopping from one city to another along the isthmus of Central America. First we landed in Panama, then in Costa Rica, next on to Nicaragua, then returning to colorful Guatemala, and finally, visiting the Yucatán Peninsula in Mexico—all of those places for a second or third time. What on earth was I thinking? That it would be easy? Angel said it would be easier to do it then than later on, and perhaps he was right. I had wanted, in particular, to see what had happened in Nicaragua since the civil war. But after relaxing in Costa Rica, I felt uneasy about landing in Managua.

It was a bittersweet reunion—me with that troubled country I had previously come to know so well. As I came off the plane in Managua, a wall of hot air threatened to knock me over again, exactly as it had two years before, this time with a baby in my arms and a toddler at my feet. Ignoring my eyes pleading for help, Angel hustled down the steps ahead of me to check on the embassy car we were borrowing. I was left, octopus-like, balancing flight bags and young children on the hot midafternoon pavement.

The merry month of May is anything but in many countries in that area of the Caribbean. In Nicaragua, the rainy season begins in earnest sometime in June. But a month or two before, there is day after day of searing and enervating heat, the air thick with humidity desperate to explode like a water balloon. Giant insects go mad with a dizzying rain dance, as much in need of water as the rest of us. And then, when the clouds finally open up in June, they continue bursting almost daily until November. The sense of relief I felt was great, many days going outside to dance in the rain like a child.

But on that brief trip, there would be no such relief for us. *Please*, I prayed, wiping the perspiration from Annie's forehead, *let there be air-conditioning in Ticomo now.* We drove to one of our first State Department houses in Managua, a little one-room cabin on the Carretera Sur. Staying there for a few short days, just long enough to see and feel the aftermath of the civil war, Angel wanted to consult with some staffers at the American embassy. I felt tethered to the needs of my little children, and the one or two friends I'd had there had fled the country before the revolution. Managua seemed strangely vacant to me—and desperately lonely.

While the children napped and Angel read cables on the patio, I lay down and sifted through the memories of two unfor-gettable years of my life: Amanda, Gloria, and Dora, three women who had provided us with indispensable household help; the last one, Dora, was Carter's nanny and loved caring for him; Angel's exciting first post in the diplomatic service, so full of promise for him; my apprenticeship in teaching at Academia Internacional; the bougainvillea exploding with color in November when the rains finally stopped.

My thoughts fell on those three women who had taken care of our house during our tour there:

They had been my first surrogate family, I remembered think-ing, *since by then I was used to not having any family around me.*

I pictured Amanda, who had barely turned eighteen when she began working for us. She left the job six months later because her family was suddenly moving north to Jinotega. They provided childcare for her two little boys, and she had to go with them. As she braced herself to tell me she was leaving, she began sobbing, and I was so moved by her tears. Working for an American family carried with it a number of benefits, and she knew what she was walking away from.

Her replacement wasted no time. Word traveled fast in her neighborhood, and within two days she was knocking on my door with her little girl.

"*Buenas tardes*, señora. My name is Gloria Rojas. Amanda Torres said you were looking for help, and I hope you will take me. A year ago, I worked for the Johnson family until they went back to Washington. The embassy has their letter of recommendation if you want to see it."

"Thank you, Gloria. C'mon in. And who is this pretty little girl?" I asked, admiring her wavy golden hair and running my fingers through it. *Gloria speaks good English. She has worked for Americans before, and she picked up the language well.*

"Marisa, señora. Isn't she beautiful?" she answered, clearly excited by my interest. "I'm so happy to have a *rubia* child! Even her eyes are gray—not black!" she boasted, beaming that her little girl had light coloring.

I'll never forget how her pride in her daughter's appearance struck me. Gloria herself was mestizo like the majority of Nicaraguans, with dark hair, eyes, and skin color. Having a white child represented, to Gloria, a gift from God.

Coming from the WASP culture of New England, it was easy for me to forget how people had traded on the color of their skin for centuries. And Gloria was no different. Marisa was her calling card wherever she went. She was ambitious for her daughter—and for herself. It therefore surprised me to see her pack up and leave with Marisa after a few short months.

My reverie continued:

It was January of 1977, and I had just become pregnant with Carter. Floating through the front door, I located her in the kitchen making her delicious *nacatamales* for the reception we were having that evening.

"Gloria, I have such good news," I said, beaming with delight. "Next fall there will be a new baby in this house. I'm so excited. Angel and I have been hoping for a baby for over a year!"

But Gloria, far from happy for me, appeared stricken.

"Really, señora? How can you be so sure?"

"I just came from the doctor's office where I had a urine test, and it was positive. Also, I have a weird taste in my mouth all the time. Cigarettes taste awful to me now, so I'm finally quitting!"

"Oh, well, it's good you're not smoking anymore. I, myself, never ever smoked cigarettes. *Muy feo*," she said, crinkling her nose. "Anyway, what time is your party starting later? I may need to go to the market to get some things."

"People will start coming around nine. Please set up everything on the tables outside," I instructed in a chilly voice, clearly miffed by her indifference to my good news. I went to my bedroom and took a shower, caressing my newly pregnant body and missing a congratulatory hug from the first person to hear my happy news.

A few days later Gloria told me she was quitting. Her explanation was that Marisa missed sleeping in her own room at her grandmother's house. At our house, she and her daughter had been sleeping in the hut in our backyard where all household help were expected to live. She probably had been hoping to move into the main house and to our guest bedroom. But now the baby would be sleeping there. And what she might have wanted wouldn't be possible. She was ambitious indeed.

Providing me with so little notice, at least she found a wonderful woman to replace her, an older woman named Dora who would prove to be a warm and loving nanny to my son.

I must have fallen asleep, but the children's noise awakened me. Now that we were back in Managua, it was Dora I sought out because she would want to see Carter.

Without the convenience of telephones, I had to drive over to her neighborhood, where I found her sitting on her front porch. She had always gone home from wherever she'd been working on Sundays, and I was happy to see her still living in the same place. Surprised and thrilled to see me after two years, Dora let her needlepoint slip from her lap into the dirt as she ran to greet me.

Her house emptied as if there had been a fire inside as everyone circled around my car to greet me. They had heard about La Señora Marilea often and were excited to meet this American lady. Shaking hands with at least ten people before making grave apologies for rushing off, I pushed Dora into the front seat and took off in a hurry.

Angel was watching the children, but soon an embassy friend would be picking him up to go to a luncheon.

It was a blisteringly hot afternoon in May. Dora enjoyed sitting in our cabin with fans blowing in every direction, drinking lemonade and eating some sweets. Watching her fuss over the little boy she had taken care of two years before and his baby sister, I knew upon my arrival in Virginia that I would dearly miss having a female companion to help me.

Dora insisted on taking the bus home, and there was a stop

across the street. She tearfully embraced the child she had watched over as an infant, and as we hugged and took leave of each other, I felt relieved to be saying goodbye to her—and to Nicaragua.

Managua seemed full of ghosts. I was anxious to get on a plane and keep going north.

LITTLE GIRL

Haunted by the Chamorro assassination, I begged Angel to request a job that would keep him in the States for as much time as the State Department would allow. I longed for the boredom of disposable diapers, Safeway, and *Sesame Street*. He agreed that we needed to establish some stability now that we had a growing family, and the State Department reassigned us to Washington for seven years.

The privilege of embassy cars and encounters with well-known people greeted us overseas, where we lived in a cocoon of advantages and comfort. In Washington, DC, we were nobody from nowhere, fending for ourselves without household help and paying our own rent.

Taxes in Virginia didn't pay for enough snowplows, so a big nor'easter could easily disrupt daily routines for weeks. But my children were little, and school wasn't an issue. I picture Annie at the top of our unplowed street, unafraid of sledding down the hill. She was always fearless, like Princess Leia battling the Stormtroopers.

What a brave little girl! What a brave little girl!

BAMBOO

In November of 1980, I felt the same symptom I'd had with all my other pregnancies: my taste buds changed, and I couldn't eat the same foods as before; my sweet tooth disappeared and I didn't like sugar. As with Carter and Annie, I often filled up on liver and spinach. The test came back positive, and our family of four prepared to be a family of five.

I came from three. My brother and sister each had three.

Angel and I were happy to be having our third child, due a little over a year after we'd returned from South America.

At four in the morning on July 19, 1981, Angel plopped sleepy Carter and Annie into the back of the station wagon, dropped me off at the hospital, and went back home.

Caroline slid into the daylight around seven in the morning, and I was home after lunch.

Spoiled from four years of help overseas, I felt assaulted by crying, demands, meals, laundry, and cleaning up after three kids under four—with no sleep—and my ever-present demons kept knocking on the door.

And I remembered Herkimer.

SHADOWS

There were periods of time when I was so lost to myself that I could have been living on the moon, my husband and children mere appendages on a sinking ship. The binge-purge cycle of eating reclaimed its prominence in my life when my young children should have taken up all of my energy.

After dropping the children off at their preschool, there were many ways to utilize those three precious hours: I might have gone shopping or to the dentist; I could have gotten a pedicure or even stayed home to wash windows. Often I did prefer to stay home, but not to do any cleaning. Some mornings I sat on my sofa staring at my mother's Swiss cuckoo clock on the wall: *click-click*, the big hand advancing slowly as I, trancelike, followed each movement. Other days the 5:35—that tired, old (binging) commuter train—still stopped at my house, and I found myself at 7-Eleven buying junk food, only to have it end up in the toilet before I had to pick up the kids.

Growing terribly restless, I closed myself off in our basement library and fantasized about having a paying job. But I felt ashamed of wanting a career.

I'm a pariah and a bad mother for wanting to do this.

Being married to an officer in the Foreign Service would limit my career choices. Even if I did get a job at one of our posts, it wouldn't last. Moving was a way of life for State Department families. But I didn't have the honesty or the courage to address my needs.

While the children were playing in the family room across the hall, sometimes heavily pummeling each other, I flipped through graduate school manuals and decided to become a social worker.

I want to help people. I always feel better about myself when I do, whether it's volunteer work or a paid position. I want to make a difference.

Did I recognize this powerful need to justify being born?

BALLOONS

With Carter, my milk flowed so poorly that he literally had to bite me with his gums to get any nourishment. My breasts were covered with bruises. Then there was the mastitis. I had two bouts of that infection before leaving Managua. And since there were only cold showers for the two years we lived there, I wasn't able to squeeze the pus out in a steaming hot shower. Nevertheless, I was determined to continue nursing until he was ready to quit.

Nursing Annie in Quito, I had the same difficulty along with two bouts of mastitis. But at least there were hot showers there.

When Caroline nursed, two bouts of mastitis plagued me, but they cleared up quickly with heat and antibiotics. I knew I'd miss nursing her, so we kept at it for eighteen months, enjoying the closeness we felt while she was at my breast.

My husband, however, was not pleased with what nursing had done to my pendulous breasts. They hung, quite literally, down to my waist.

"Marilea," he said, staring at my breasts as though he were shopping for a tie, "I think you should get a breast lift. I think you'd be much happier with your appearance if you weren't practically hanging down to the floor." He smiled at me, but his smile couldn't cover up the idea that I was like a tie he would not have selected.

Who would be happier, Angel, you or me? You're the one who needs me to be attractive. I look like a woman who's birthed and nursed three children. I'm trying to be happy just as I am.

Those words did not find their way to my vocal chords.

"All right, Angel. But it will take me about six months to wean Caroline. I'll nurse her for the last time on her second birthday. Then I'll have the operation."

He didn't like my waiting so long. But it was important for me to wean my little girl slowly.

To get back at me, he withdrew his affection for a long time. He was used to getting his own way, and he was angry. Despite jumping through hoops in other ways to please him, I was resolute.

WAIT

The phone rang in the library downstairs.

"Marilea," my sister spoke slowly. "I have such terrible news. Daddy has died. It was sudden. He had a massive coronary at home today, and," she said, her voice breaking, "he died in the hospital a few hours later. They couldn't do anything to save him."

"Oh God, no," I cried, sobbing into the phone, "and I couldn't be there! I didn't get to say goodbye to him!"

"None of us did, Marilea. He went quickly."

"What will you do now?"

"We'll plan the funeral and burial in a few days."

"No, I need to see him first. I need to see my father before you bury him."

"Marilea, let's all get together and talk about what to do. How soon can you get up here?"

"I'll leave the kids with my girlfriend in the babysitting co-op. I know she'll keep them until I come back. I'll catch the next flight. Don't do anything until I get there."

"Call me when you know your arrival time. Maybe Bill can get you at the airport."

My father was cremated, but not before he'd been embalmed and there was a viewing. I stood on one side of his body while my sister faced me on the other side.

ICEBERGS

Though I'd longed for it, my siblings and I were not close. I'd moved away from Massachusetts years before, and despite my efforts to visit when I was in the country, it was difficult to span the emotional distance during our brief visits.

Once I told my sister how much I loved to watch *Ben-Hur*.

"Oh, yes," she agreed, sighing, "always the happy endings."

And she said it with a little sadness, as though she'd been disappointed at times too.

What an ocean of information we'd neglected to share with one another all those years. I wish we could have been closer to each other.

We're not so different, my sister and I. We're just two ships that sailed on the same stormy sea, landing far away from each other.

SOLO

"You can't come in, Carter. We're playing with our dolls!" Annie and Caroline shouted as they locked the bedroom door, shutting him out.

Ever since they were preschoolers, the same scene played itself out in my young family. I don't understand why they behaved that way, but I do know that intervention was called for. My son was in a lot of pain and I was passive.

"Let them work it out themselves," the pediatrician said when I told him how I worried.

They worked it out. Annie and Caroline had been close ever since they were little, and Carter had been an only child.

His preschool teachers said he was aggressive. So Angel and I put him on sports teams three seasons a year.

Unaware of how angry he was, I thought he just loved sports.

WITNESS

So there you have it—my sorry tale.
That's how something I thought I controlled
ended up controlling me.

—Sarah Darer Littman[11]

"**M**om, what were you doing in the bathroom? I was calling you from the basement." Annie was clearly upset by something. "Didn't you hear us come home from school?"

"I felt sick from the banquet they served us in Charlottesville. Too much rich food," I lied, embarrassed that she must have heard my retching.

Instead of starting a career, I had taken a volunteer job in a program at the Woodburn Center for Mental Health. I wrote a proposal to fund a support group for women's mental health:

If vulnerability to mental illness were measured, women at home with young children would top the scale. The isolation of living in a big decentralized geographical area with a large percentage of the population in a mobile state, where unemployment is high and competition for the few good jobs left is even higher, is terrible. There are pressures to living in the Washington, DC, area that are unique and render the women trying to adjust to living here susceptible to depression, among other things. Informal groups of women have been forming at the grassroots level for several years in northern Virginia in the hopes of meeting precisely this need.

The volunteer coordinator at Woodburn accepted my proposal, and we began setting up a twice-monthly support group for women, facilitated by a licensed clinical social worker. We structured the meetings around a set of topics we could all relate to, and it was an enjoyable outlet for stay-at-home moms like myself. My supervisor felt such pride in my efforts that she nominated me to be recognized by the Virginia Mental Health and Mental Retardation Board in the spring of 1986. We drove to Charlottesville together to receive the award in May.

In a framed picture, I am shaking hands with the presenter as she hands me my award, wearing my white Easter suit and offering a dazzling smile in all that heady company receiving other distinguished honors. Inside, I am sweating profusely and wondering how soon I can get back to my kitchen to lose the torturous war between healthy self-esteem and self-loathing.

I should have been glowing with pride. In my own small way, I had made a difference to several housewives in my area, and support groups like the one I had started were becoming popular. But I wasn't able to accept that honor and feel good about myself. I arrived home from Charlottesville carrying my framed "Best Volunteer of the Year" award, flung it across the hardwood floor of my living room, entered the kitchen, and flailed around looking for whatever junk food I could find. Then I purged in the bathroom.

That was my response to being celebrated for my work.

My coveted award was lying on the living room floor inside

an eight-by-ten-inch frame, the glass shattered into many pieces, a disturbing reflection of how I felt about myself.

"Carter was kicking me. You never make him stop!" Annie cried, fighting back the tears.

I retreated to a familiar place: intense dissatisfaction with my life, my mothering, myself.

"Work it out yourselves," I wearily told her, lying down on my bed. "I'm tired from my trip."

Another locked door. Another unavailable mother.

ON THE EDGE

C oming from the largely patriarchal society of Cuba, Angel fully expected to be in charge in our marriage. The two of us clashed more and more on big and little things. I wanted the kids to learn to love the outdoors as I did growing up. After Angel agreed to buy a tent, all five of us went camping one weekend in West Virginia.

But it was a disaster. It wasn't an adventure for him; he wasn't in his element, and he knew it. Nor did he have any interest in learning.

"No more camping," he ordered.

His decision to put an end to camping was nonnegotiable. In an effort to have peace, I went along with him.

My resentment began chipping away at the foundation of our marriage. I pushed it down—stuffed it like many food addicts would.

I conceded on one decision after another. Angel also loved going out in the evening, but I was tired by dinnertime and hated leaving the kids with sitters. Still, I agreed to go, angry much of the time. A therapist I would see a few years later told me I had been saving up a lot of chips.

"Deal from strength" is a well-worn maxim, but too often fear gets in the way. Fear of abandonment, fear of failure, fear of attention, and, oh dear, fear of inattention—had allowed me to call my choices into question over the years.

What was I afraid of losing? Who was I afraid of offending? Who, in fact, was that nebulous human being playing by other people's rules because she didn't speak her own mind or know what she wanted out of life?

I was still trying to please my mother—and had married a man who was so much like her.

When we were first married, I didn't mind Angel's dominance at all. But at some point, after we'd returned to the States from South America, I did start to mind. I was changing and wasn't sure how to negotiate my needs and desires within the boundaries of our marriage. I was morphing into someone else.

Our time in Virginia was coming to an end, and we were assigned to Athens, Greece, for our next post. Back overseas on the government tab to Europe and other European countries. Angel's career plan.

But what about my career plans?

Foreign Service posts involved two- or three-year assignments. Families couldn't fall in love with a place and decide to live there forever. It was a nomadic way of life, and it wasn't possible for wives of officers to have careers unless they were brief and perhaps transferrable.

I concluded after daydreaming those seven years in Virginia that I wanted to continue what I'd started in Nicaragua: to be a teacher and stay in one school long enough to establish friendships, learn the craft, and feel the satisfaction of growing in the profession. I had so much inside bursting to get out. Puerto Rico and Nicaragua were fortuitous experiences that planted a seed in me, and I wanted to see it come to fruition.

But I couldn't realize that dream as a high-level diplomatic wife. Deeply unhappy and too afraid at that point to do anything about it, I hoped I could put my dream on hold and make this transition successfully. Plans for the transatlantic move had already been set in motion.

STEALTH BOMBER

One weekend before we left the country, telling Angel he was on his own with the kids, I drove east to be by the sea. In Ocean City, I got a cheap hotel room and a cheap bottle of vodka, and spent my time numbing myself. Instead of walking on the beach by the ocean I love so much, instead of grabbing a bag and adding more souvenirs to my beautiful collection, I lay on my bed, drank vodka straight out of the bottle, and passed out.

I might as well have stayed in a cheap motel near my own house.

In a fog most of the time, eating junk food from the boardwalk, I ran away from my life. I left my "shell" for the weekend, ventured off by myself, as empty coming out of a bottle as I was going into it.

I learned nothing, gained nothing from escaping for a few days other than missing my children terribly. I was still as hollow as the bleached whelks waiting to be snatched up by grateful collectors.

I would discover, many years down the road, the sneaky and devastating nature of addictive disease: how it stalks you, dupes you into thinking you're okay "if it's just once in a while." It's like any virus: it needs a host to take root. And grow.

To flourish. And continue.

Addiction, like any cancer, wants to survive. It filled my empty shell, opportunistic disease that it is, with false confidence, false promises, false hopes.

Maybe I'll be happier in Greece . . .

CROSSROADS

It's hard to see which of the many turning points in my life was the most important. I usually avoided the more difficult paths. Many times, I made choices that were easy: the pill to feel better, the food in my mouth, the isolation that dwarfed and limited me, the subservience to my husband. But the juncture that changed my life forever occurred during the three years we were living in Greece: 1987–90. That was the stage for a fundamental and lasting change in me, where I started to wake up and question who I was and what I wanted to do in my life.

When I arrived there, I was ready for it.

ELENI

The American embassy moved us into a handsome three-story house in a northern suburb of Athens called Politia. At the end of my street where the kids picked up their school bus were two or three stores, including a beauty salon. I peeked in there one day and asked if the hairdresser could fit me in. Thus began a thirty-year friendship that defies explanation. We had absolutely nothing in common, but we had an affinity for one another that is rare.

Eleni became my closest friend, and in addition to having my hair done regularly, I learned what platonic love between women was meant to be. In a country that is so defined by love that there are several different words for it—*philia*, the love between friends; *eros*, or sexual love; and *agape*, a love for all people, often defined as charity—Eleni and I, straight women, both married with children, cared deeply for one another.

She invited me one or two evenings a week to her home for dinner. Dinner for Greeks is a grand affair, and the more people the better. Starting at nine or ten o'clock, a first course might be put on the table, followed by several more courses, with cigarettes in between. After a ten-year hiatus from smoking while I was pregnant and nursing, I had returned to that destructive habit. It was easy in Greece where everyone seemed to be smoking.

There's nothing lonelier to a Greek than being alone at meal-time. At Eleni's, I added more place settings as people continued coming. Each guest added to the joy and merriment of their dinners.

"Marilea, this is Stavroula, Ilias's mother." Ilias lived in a house behind us and ran the grocery at the end of the street next to Eleni's beauty salon. The neighborhood we lived in was like an extended family.

We talked about everything and nothing. It was the company and the food that made it an event. Eleni brought out a huge plate of baked eggplant soaked in olive oil, with black Kalamata olives and a delectable bitter cheese I never learned the name of. Her husband, Nondas, poured the Greek wine from a copper-colored pitcher into small, juice-size glasses. There were about three of those pitchers on the long table, and he made sure everyone's glass was full.

Next came a thick sirloin that is a treat for working-class Greeks. Meat on the Attican peninsula is expensive, and so is fish. Eleni and Nondas, like all the Greeks I was coming to know, were hospitable and generous.

I spent most of my time with Eleni at her home over the dinner hour. Only once did I brave the *bouzoukia*, the popular nightclubs with *laiko* music. After dinner one evening around midnight, when I would normally fall into bed, Eleni and her husband took me to one of those clubs. Trying to keep my eyes open until five in the morning, I'd never before seen a people so immersed in pleasure for its own sake, drinking and dancing away the realities many were forced to wake up to the next day.

"Eleni, you've been working your whole life. You've always been fulfilled in your career. I want to pick up the teaching career I started in Nicaragua."

MARILEA C. RABASA

"Then why don't you?"

"Because the State Department moves us around every two or three years. I can't stay in one place long enough for it to be satisfying."

She listened, nodding.

"Angel and I fight all the time now. We've really grown apart. I'm not sure I love him anymore," I admitted, breaking down in tears. "The only way I can have the career I dream about is by divorcing him and moving back to Virginia."

My friend just put her arms around me. She could see the choice in front of me.

Eleni never said much; she just listened.

She was a terrific teacher.

BUGS

Caroline's first-grade teacher looked at me with such derision. *Did she do this often, protect her little charges from their neglectful parents?*

"Mrs. Rabasa, I'm sorry to be telling you this, but your little girl has a bad case of lice. She is constantly itching her scalp and seems overly tired, like she hasn't been sleeping well. Were you aware of any of this?"

"Well, no, of course not!" Mortified, I didn't know what else to say.

"Um, how often do you bathe her?" She seemed a little embarrassed. "There's a good chance that if her hair were washed regularly, lice wouldn't have a chance to get infested there."

There it was: I neglected my child; I didn't bathe her enough.

"Oh, I feel terrible about this. What can I do right now?"

"First, I suggest cutting off all her hair. Don't worry—it'll grow back." She smiled and added, "Then go to the embassy doctor and get the medicine they prescribe."

"Okay, thanks. I wish I'd been more aware," I said, shaking my head.

"Kids often don't complain, especially if they don't think they'll be heard." I felt her boring into me with her judgment.

"I'll certainly be more careful from now on," I said, looking down at the floor. I felt about as small as the lice in my daughter's hair—and deeply ashamed of myself. "Thank you for your concern."

"Oh," she added, as I was going out the door, "and don't forget to bathe her more regularly." She was smiling as though it were funny, trying to make light of it.

I didn't think it was funny. Driving home, I was fuming.

Dragging my little girl to Eleni's at the corner, my friend chopped off all her hair while Caroline screamed.

At the grocery next door, Stavroula offered a comforting hug to Caroline and gave her a treat. I had one too. Several. We stopped off at the bakery on the other side of the beauty shop, and, remembering how Angel loved the baklava from there and the creamy custard, *galaktoboureko*, I bought enough of both for a family of eight and walked home with Caroline. She was too upset for dinner and went straight to bed. While Angel was preparing steaks for us on our indoor grill, I went down to the privacy of the basement with a glass of orange juice and several dessert portions.

With every thrust down my throat, I could hear my little girl screaming.

GLUE

S oon after we arrived in Greece, we added a wonderful one-
year-old mixed breed Labrador to our family. He was a salve
for our wounded children. Surely, they had heard Angel and me
quarreling over the past year or two and must have been worried.
But Oscar was their refuge, especially Annie's.

I smile at the dry sense of humor she expressed in poems she
wrote:

"A Dog's Point of View"

They give me the same food every day
Which I'm very tired of.
And they give me dirty looks
From way up above.
When I beg at the table
They scold me.
If they didn't want me to
They really should have told me.
They give me cold baths
Way outside
When they get a nice warm tub.
And they tell me to get lost
When all I want is a belly rub.

They make me sleep
At the foot of their bed,
So I have to stare at toes.
And they make these strange sounds at night
Usually coming out of their nose!

Though I have drawers full of cards and gifts she'd made me over the years, physical displays of affection were difficult for her, and she wasn't a hugger.

Not so with Oscar. She bathed him, groomed him, walked him, and slept with him until the day he died thirteen years later. He found an opening in her, a vulnerability, that would remind me, years later, what a beautiful soul had always resided in my daughter.

The children took care of all his needs: fed him, walked him, played ball with him, and tried to train him not to nip at people. Oscar flew across the Atlantic with us in the baggage compartment because we couldn't bear to be apart from him during one summer vacation. That dog looked like death, shaking and sweating like a newborn calf, when we got him at the airport.

"There he is, Mom!" Annie shouted, running toward the handlers as they opened the animal cages. "Oscar!" My little girl who never cried had tears in her eyes.

And Oscar was jumping all over her, happy to see us all.

STRAWS

Our first year in Greece, Angel and I took the kids swimming on Crete, went skiing at Mount Parnassus, and made the trip up to Nea Makri Naval Base often to buy things in the commissary. There were four bases in Greece that we used for our shopping: the large Hellenikon Air Base, just south of Athens; the small one north of us on the island of Evia; and two more bases on Crete, one in Souda Bay and another in Iraklion. The American presence in that country was considerable and was becoming more and more controversial.

In a letter to my mother, dated 11/24/87, I wrote:

Dear Mom,

Angel has been on the front page of the news here. He has been on the negotiating team for the American bases here. He was in London and Stuttgart for a week, meeting Ambassador Flanagan, and brought him here to begin negotiations with the Greeks. The whole process will be on and off for a couple of years. I'm sure Angel will be promoted as a result of this. Now that his picture was on the front page, we will be hotly pursued by the Greeks. Security has to be increased now. Angel and I have to switch cars occasionally.

I took more of an interest in the political controversy with the unfolding of a tragedy in my own neighborhood—the place where my children had roamed around freely, walking their dog, playing ball, and feeling entirely safe.

As that first school year ended, our family was busy squabbling over what our summer plans would be. But all the plans came to a sudden halt on June 28 with the assassination of our neighbor Bill Nordeen.

US Attaché Killed in Athens: Bomb in Parked Car Set Off as Officer Leaves His Home on Way to Embassy
JUNE 28, 1988
12 A.M.
FROM TIMES WIRE SERVICES
ATHENS—

The US military attaché in Greece was killed today on the street where he lived by a remote-control bomb in a parked car. The blast blew his armor-plated auto off the road as he drove to work.

The officer, identified by the US embassy as Navy Capt. William E. Nordeen, 51, was decapitated and thrown about ten yards from his car, witnesses said.

No one immediately claimed responsibility for the blast, but suspicions fell on leftist groups that have terrorized American military personnel in Greece in recent years.[12]

This was too close.

A security detail drove Angel to work daily following the murder, and I shook with fear for months, thinking of my children walking to the school bus every day. Pedro Joaquín Chamorro had been murdered in Nicaragua only ten years before. Up until that second murder, I had enjoyed a devil-may-care attitude about my life. Our adventures in the Foreign Service had been enriching and stimulating—but also dangerous. Even with the kids, I eventually went along, firmly attached to my husband and the sexiness he found from living on the edge.

Angel was attracted to danger; it's true. It's not accidental that he became a terrorism expert at the Rand Corporation following his tenure in the Foreign Service. And I think when we were first married, it felt exhilarating, watching the fomenting of a left-wing revolution in Nicaragua. I was younger then, and I didn't have a growing family to consider.

I didn't find the edge exhilarating anymore.

My husband was relaxed and unstressed about the work challenges he was dealing with and the threats to Americans. But it was a difficult time for me. Our house had become an armed camp with policemen guarding our comings and goings.

"Angel, why is the security detail here all the time? It's scaring the children," I asked him as I watched our kids running to catch the bus. My hands had begun to shake—my reaction to fear that went back to my childhood. "I don't want to see police cars here all the time. Please, can't you tell them to meet you at the corner?"

"Stop it, Marilea," he snapped, brushing me off, "do you want to end up a widow like your mother?"

I woke up one night while Angel was away on embassy business, sweating and shaking, with the image of heads on stakes up and down the highway to the base at Nea Makri. I doubled the number of cigarettes I'd been smoking in an effort to relieve my stress.

The children were in school all day and had many after-school activities to occupy themselves. But I couldn't sleep much at night, continually waking with old "They're coming to get me" nightmares from my 1973 breakdown so many years before. But there in Greece it wasn't drug-induced paranoia: those fears were real. The terrorist organization under suspicion, November 17, had promised to kill more American diplomats if the United States refused to remove its bases from Greece.

The bomb that blew up near our house that day was still exploding in me.

Every time I saw Angel's security guard pick him up, I wondered if he'd be coming home that night.

Bill Nordeen had also been in an armor-plated vehicle, and it did nothing to protect him.

ECHO

That summer Annie found a newborn kitten abandoned on the sidewalk on the way home from the corner store.

"Mom," she said, excited and out of breath, "I found this kitty on the sidewalk. Can I please keep it? It's really dirty, and I want to give it a bath."

She ran up to her bathroom and filled the tub with water.

Before I could get upstairs to stop her, Annie had that kitten in the bathtub. She was nine years old, and she didn't understand how a lot of water could harm a newborn kitten. Oscar loved being soaked with water.

Frantic to get the kitten out of the tub, I pushed Annie out of the way, grabbed the kitten in a blanket, and lay down on the bed with it, trying to warm it up. I did all I could to revive it, but its lungs were full of water. I felt it heaving, struggling, but the poor thing couldn't breathe.

That kitty died in my arms while Annie lay on the bed on the other side of me.

"Annie, it got pneumonia. It was too little and weak for me to save it." I felt myself slipping back in time and started crying.

"Mom, I'm sorry." Her voice broke, but she didn't shed any tears. "I didn't know it'd get pneumonia. I just wanted a kitty to play with Oscar."

"I know, honey," I said, sympathetic then for her loss as well. "Let's dig a little hole in the rose garden and bury it there." Annie solemnly carried the little corpse outside and laid it in the grass while I dug a hole with my gardener's trowel. I reached for her hand after we buried the kitten, but she brushed me off and ran into the house to play with Oscar. I wanted to be a protective wall against her pain and hurt, but I, too, felt the pain of this loss as I revisited my eight-year-old self in the house by the lake. How many kittens had I buried when I was Annie's age?

Our family animals had been my principal source of affection: Herkimer and all her babies, Hugo, and Corky.

Bill was so much older than me, and he moved away when I was only five years old. Lucy was closer to me in age, but we had few shared interests.

In our house—when I wasn't escaping to one of my outside homes—it was my animals that gave me a sense of peace, acceptance, wholeness, and above all, unconditional love. Annie was gratified in the same way through Oscar.

I felt such a connection to my young daughter in that moment, as she'd found another outlet for her affection only to have it taken away from her. I recalled the incident from when I was Annie's age and I lost two of Herkimer's newborn kittens. Had I foreseen the gruesome sight awaiting me on the screen porch that morning, I might have taken steps to protect Herkie's newborns from the crushing weight of our German shepherd, Hugo. I felt guilty then but kept my feelings to myself. And I didn't want my little girl to feel responsible for what had happened to the kitten, either. We both tended to keep our feelings deep inside us, fearing retribution and not trusting in good outcomes or, often, the people around us.

Our love of animals filled a large space in our hearts, and it appeared now as though my daughter and I were starting to mirror one another.

RUMBLINGS

Down in the basement of our large three-story house, I regularly retreated to the isolation of food binges: stuffing my stomach with an uncomfortable amount of Greek food, usually the *galaktoboureko* from the corner bakery or baklava, dripping with honey, washed down with hot tea or juice. Then the "unstuffing" portion of the ritual, a critical part, because purging and the flat tummy I enjoyed afterward fed the illusion that I could get away with the behavior, that there would be few consequences—a shortsighted attitude, one that most addicts indulge in.

Of course there were consequences: money spent on wasted food; time spent away from the children sneaking around in the basement; more damage to my teeth; more self-loathing; and guilt, my old nemesis, continuing to undermine my ability to be a strong parent, which I needed then more than ever as the turbulence around me increased: the political assassination, a failed marriage spinning out of control, and my children surely feeling the effects of all this unraveling.

THE TRAIN

The following summer, I wrote a cable to the State Department with a proposal for a mental health grant to serve our embassy community. Similar to the idea I'd had in northern Virginia, I asked for a small amount of money to hire a trained therapist to facilitate a support group of embassy wives. Included in the proposal was a stipend for myself for doing the organizing and writing quarterly reports to the State Department.

My proposal was accepted. The money I had asked for came through along with a small office to work in.

"Good job, Marilea! Something like this couldn't have come at a better time!" the secretary enthused.

"I agree. Let's hope it will help out our community. And thanks!"

I wrote to my mother on 9/30/89:

Dear Mom,

My good news is that I was awarded the job I applied for: mental health grant coordinator, a one-year contract position. I am thrilled to have this job, not only because it will be fun to do but also because I got it solely on the basis of all the years of volunteer work I've done—no social work degree or other academic qualifications.

All those years of volunteer work seem to have paid off, even in this small way. Thank you so much for introducing me to service work when I was thirteen! Your insight and guidance pointed me in the right direction a number of times. I'm really hoping the program I plan on starting will help the embassy wives here. There's so much isolation in the American community.

I found a local professional to act as facilitator, and we got organized quickly. Once it got going, the program enjoyed a successful yearlong tenure. When I wasn't at the support group, I was spending time with Eleni and her family. It also felt good to have my own office where I spent a few mornings a week. Angel, too, was away a lot, throwing himself into his work and his interest in terrorism. He supported my working part-time. For both of us that year, work filled the void in our unhappy marriage. At ages eight, ten, and twelve years old, though, the children were too often alone.

I started pulling away.

Where was I going?

God, I had three children at home who needed me.

Like a train that had left the station, I wasn't there for them.

WIDOW

A widow for two years, my mother came to live with us for three months every spring during our tour in Greece. Greek Easter is a grand affair, and Eleni welcomed my mother into her home for the lamb feast and celebration.

In all the years they had been married, my parents had only traveled abroad once or twice. My father hated to travel, and that was another resentment my mother stockpiled like weapons in her arsenal.

She had been, for much of the time, unhappily married to my father for forty-nine and a half years. They'd eloped soon after they'd met, barely knowing one another. My mother would soon discover that she had married an alcoholic, and we all watched as her pleading and martyrdom often made her appear sad and bitter.

His death was a great shock to her, and it took her a while to get her bearings. However, it also gave her the freedom to travel she'd long given up hoping for.

When I invited her to come live with us, she couldn't believe her good luck.

Mother was happy because she loved the classics and enjoyed being able to live in the land of Homer and Sophocles. Her visits gave the children many opportunities to further bond with their grandmother. And I was grateful to have a loving presence in the house when I was too distracted with work and other things to be a strong parent for my children.

She often filled in for me making dinner for the children.

"Pot roast again, Nana?" Carter whined. "Can't we have burgers?"

"Maybe tomorrow. Your mother is going shopping today at Nea Makri and said she'll bring home some ground beef, right, Marilea?" she asked, looking my way. "Can't you wait that long, Carter?" Mother turned and offered a hug to her grandson as he smiled in anticipation.

"Sure, Nana," he said, returning the hug. Leaving the kitchen, he turned and added, "I'm so glad you're staying with us now. I always miss you when you go."

"Oh, Carter, it's so nice to hear you say that!"

"One more thing, Marilea," she added, catching me as I was leaving, "please remember veggie patties for Annie. She really loves them."

"Sure, Mom, if they're in stock at the commissary. Bye!"

I'm glad she never fought me on the name change—never, not once. I got into my car, musing about my crashing into puberty. *Mary Lee.* I hated that southern name, and even more so how she just called me "Mary" instead. How would most mothers feel if their daughters decided that the name they had chosen was pretty dull and that they wanted to improve upon it, tweak it, make it more interesting? Would those mothers be offended? Have them evaluated? Sent away? I was only twelve—and she would rule me in the years to come in more ways than I'd like to remember—but I got my way on that one.

My mother was often overcome with guilt around my upbringing. She spoke of it on many occasions.

In her recollections, in her voice's wistful tone, in her reaching for my hands, Mother was asking for my forgiveness.

That knowing resonated with me on an unconscious level, and among her letters after she died, I found a note I had written that year when she was with us in Greece:

Dear Mom,

There comes a time (and your time is long overdue) when we all have to come to terms with our lives as we have seen fit to live them. It takes courage to say, "Okay, these are the roads I've chosen, these are the choices I've made, these are my failures, these are my victories, but I can live with myself." And then let it go. Actually, I think you're more at peace with yourself than you realize.

Was I writing that letter to myself thirty years ago and addressing it to my mother? I discovered more entries in her Greek diary after she died:

During the three years that Marilea's family lived in Greece, I spent three months each spring in that hauntingly beautiful country. I took several tours, covering all of southern Greece, and found that the best way to see several islands was by cruise ship. I must mention that from the cruise ships, the little villages on the hillsides are picturesque; climbing up the stony inclines, each village had a church, sparkling white with a blue dome . . . the clear air in Greece—unlike anywhere else in the world—lavender mountains . . . turquoise sea . . .

When I was at M's house, I used to go every afternoon to meet the children at the bus. They had to cross a busy, dangerous street, but they darted across without waiting for my hands.

Hair done, packed, I watched the sunset over the mountain for the last time from the balcony. Annie said she will miss watching the sunset with me, taking walks, and having me braid her hair. My darling Annie . . .

I've read *Necessary Losses* three times. I already am prepared for death, but hope it's a few years away . . .

M's very restless and moody. At the airport, she put her arm around me and thanked me for coming just now when she needed me . . . Carter said "Bye" and then hugged me and then turned to me and hugged me again <u>very hard</u>. I am sad to leave them. M wants me to come again in the fall. I don't know . . . maybe.

I had been ready then to confide in her about how unhappy I was in my marriage. I believe she supported me so I wouldn't make the same mistake she had made: staying with her husband for the sake of the children. She felt I had suffered the most growing up, and said that sometimes she'd wished she'd had the courage to leave my father. She'd even packed a suitcase once. But those were different times; separation would be easier for me. That spring of 1990, her last trip to Greece, I tearfully told her my decision.

"Mom," I started out, holding her hands in mine, "Angel and I have been unhappy for a long time. I haven't wanted to burden you with all the details these past few years, but when Bill Nordeen was murdered two years ago, and so close to our house, it really shook me up and brought a lot of things to the surface, things I hadn't been able to look at before."

"Like what, dear?" she asked. We'd never had a close mother-daughter relationship, one where I could turn to her with my problems. I'd always tried to keep up appearances, more than ever after I'd married and become the diplomat's wife she was so proud of.

A few years earlier, before we went to Greece, Angel and I brought the kids to Massachusetts from Virginia for a visit. In a conversation I won't forget, Mother called a friend of hers to meet us:

"Bea, can you come over after lunch? Marilea is visiting with her husband and children, and I want you to meet him. He's a diplomat with the State Department, you know, and they lived in Quito, Ecuador. Sid and I visited there soon after their daughter Annie was born, and it's the most beautiful country! I can't wait to see where they'll go next. Angel is rising fast, from what Marilea tells me."

But there was so much more to me, shameful and embarrassing things, that my mother knew nothing of. I realize now that I enjoyed sitting on the pedestal where my mother had placed me at that time in my life. She was only too happy to forget the lost years of my childhood and adolescence, my obesity, and my emotional instability. I was prideful but deceitful, holding on to my elevated position by concealing what was really going on with me behind closed doors. My closet had housed a colorful collection of masks.

"I just don't want to be married to a man who invites danger the way he does," I continued. "He loves it. He's excited by it. But I'm terrified," I said, remembering the night of the murder, when Angel was brought home in a security detail. "I want to go back to Virginia where I'll feel safer." As much as she loved and admired Angel, she feared for the children as well.

My mother stood up abruptly, went to pick up a piece of trash on the floor, and placed it in the wastebasket. She looked completely calm, as though she knew where the conversation were going and welcomed it.

"What will you do now?" She turned to face me.

"I want to get a divorce." I spoke with conviction.

Without skipping a beat, she said casually, "Oh, everybody gets divorced," as though it weren't a big deal, as though she could accept it.

It took me a moment to register her response. "Come back and sit down, Mother," I said, smiling and turning our attention to the piano. "Look at how pretty the fringed red shawl looks on top with the family photos. I'm so glad I refinished your piano that summer after Daddy died." I touched it to show how much I admired the work that went into it. "It's hard to believe you paid twenty-five dollars for it in 1955!" It felt good to share the praise with the woman who had been the hypercritical parent, who'd scrutinized everything about me as long as I could remember, the woman who'd kept me bound to her wrist like a rubber band and when I'd rebelled, pulled on it so it snapped, stinging me.

That woman.

Who had she become in her eightieth year?

In that moment, my heart was so full. I felt at home with my mother for the first time in my life.

"Marilea, you'll be fine," she said as she sat down beside me. "Whatever you decide to do, you'll be fine. I have great confidence in your abilities," she concluded, reaching for my hands.

And I believed her.

All I felt just then was gratitude that my mother and I had arrived at such a comfortable place. It was there in Greece, at that terrible crossroads in my life, that we began to heal what had been a painful and complicated relationship.

Her support and the gap she filled in my children's lives at that time were a gift. She became another one of my miracles.

On 1/9/91, she wrote:

Happy Birthday, dear one. I love and admire you for all your accomplishments, and through thick and thin, good times and bad, you've always tried to put your family first. I know it wasn't always easy. You have raised three wonderful children who are a credit to you, and you have taught them to pay attention to their grandparents. At this point in my life, that is so important to me!

I send you special love,

Mother

The end of my marriage would be a critical test for me, and though I said nothing at the time to Angel or the children, I knew there was no turning back. But what a joy to be able to appreciate the silver lining in the unfolding events: a peace between my mother and me that we had been unable to achieve before.

Perhaps someday I would be able to stop holding back the truths that shamed me. For now, having her blessing to do what I needed to do was profoundly nurturing.

BLOSSOM

Since Annie was three years old, I had gotten on the Beltway in Virginia at five o'clock to get her to Mr. Youseffi's gymnastics class. Twice a week. During rush hour.

Sometimes I left Carter and Caroline with one of the other mothers in my babysitting cooperative, but not always. Carter was five, and Caroline, at one, was still nursing. My son brought his Legos, and I kept my toddler close. Annie blossomed through the physical challenges of gymnastics.

In Greece, though, she really took off. At eight, she displayed the most skill of anyone on her school gymnastics team. Annie's best friend, Jane, was also on the team, and much of my driving during our tour there involved going back and forth to Jane's so they could practice together.

Annie's work in gymnastics took her to a place where she felt competent and in control. I was not surprised when, at ten, the two girls were chosen to represent the school team at a competition in England. They didn't win a prize, but they came back laughing and more bonded than ever.

On the ride home from the airport, the girls recalled a kid from Romania whose tights had split, exposing his groin.

"Did you see the look on Dimitri's face, Janie? We could see everything! He was so embarrassed, I thought he would fall off the beam!"

I can still hear my daughter's bright belly laugh.

RECKONING

"Angel, I don't want to be married to you anymore. Too much has happened. And this isn't new. We've been unhappy for a long time. I'm just not willing to go on like this, pretending to be happy in public and coming home at night with no desire to be with you. Why won't you accept that it's over?" It wasn't the first time I'd said the words, but all the other times he'd walked away and left the room, as though it would erase the problem.

"Marilea, stop it. You knew our life would be difficult in the Foreign Service. You never objected to anything before."

"We have three children now. I've lived through two assassinations—first in Nicaragua and now in my own neighborhood—and I know how you're attracted to danger. It would be just like you to accept another hardship post for the extra money." I got nastier as I was feeling cornered.

"Okay," he offered too quickly, "I promise we'll just live in safe countries. Marilea, please, let's give us another chance. I don't want to lose you."

A broken tile at our feet caught his attention for a moment. Then he raised his gaze, looked me right in the eyes, and added defiantly, "And I don't like to lose."

So that's what this boils down to—a power struggle! I was furious.

"It's too late. There's also the teaching career I've wanted to continue for a decade now. I thought I'd be content with having the children, but it's important for me to work as well. I want to go back to teaching full-time."

There it was: the wall.

THE CONTINUOUS
LIE

The battle to keep up appearances unnecessarily,
the mask—whatever name you give creeping
perfectionism—robs us of our energies.

—Robin Worthington[13]

There was the outside Marilea: the pretty face, the strivings at work, the good mother, the good daughter, the diplomat's wife; and then there was the inside Marilea: the substance user—at one point diet pills, still food on a regular basis, and also alcohol. I kept all of this inside, my secret behavior driven by fear and insecurity building another wall between my husband and me. On one hot summer day, I retreated behind it:

"Angel, I'm tired and need to lie down. Can you take the kids to the commissary without me?"

"Sure. And since we'll be down there, they might want to go to the beach afterward. Cool off from the heat."

"That would be great. Thanks. And don't forget the paper towels."

After they got their swimsuits and towels and hugged Oscar, the kids all piled into the car and Angel drove off. I waved goodbye, happy to walk back into an empty house. Binging and purging:

that was on my agenda, not lying down. In between those episodes, I was starving myself on some days, trying to lose a few pounds.

Bulimia is a monstrous addiction. Unlike a drug I have to buy from someone, I have the means to indulge in it by myself. For many men and women, precisely because of that, it's a habit that is difficult to break.

For the fifteen years of our marriage, my husband and I enjoyed little intimacy. Back at Harvard I had my breakdown while Angel was far away in Colombia. When he came back and we got engaged, it was as though it had never happened. All these years later I had not changed in my inability to be honest with those most important to me, much less in my ability to trust that they would love me despite my flaws. I still covered up what I felt were unattractive and unacceptable parts of me. It was a lonely place for me to be, isolated by shame and stigma.

If my friends knew what I'd been hiding, they might exert pressure on me to get help. My husband was no different. And I lacked the sure-footedness and confidence to believe that he would love me, warts and all.

The only relief I felt at that point in my life was my ability to embrace some level of independence. My addictions and the soul-sickness fueling them would continue to haunt me until I could find the courage to look at myself in the mirror and shed my masks.

Until I could be honest and brave.

AIR CURRENTS

Carter and I had been driving home from his friend Chris's house one Saturday afternoon. Chris lived near Mount Pentelicus, one of my favorite haunts outside of Athens. From the crest of this hill on a clear day in winter, you could see the whole bowl of Athens with the smog hovering overhead. This was where the Brits came to celebrate Boxing Day every December 26.

Crowds of people also came to fly kites on Mount Pentelicus in December when the weather changed. As we turned the corner, we saw the tail of a kite peeking out from under a pile of rubbish, flags zigzagging down the string. Its owners must have had no more use for it when it lost its wind, and so it lay abandoned in the field.

Our curiosity taking over, we stopped the car, got out, and went to investigate. We wanted to breathe new life into this broken and tattered kite. I never thought that something inanimate could come to life. But at that time in my life, there was a dying in me that I knew I had to defeat or it would defeat me. My son was part of this tragedy, and somehow we knew that the road to healing could start with repairing that kite and watching it fly again. A dust-covered old TV pinning it down to the ground was holding the kite hostage. Its colorful tail saved it from certain death.

So we took the kite home and repaired it with glue and tape. We waited for a day with just enough wind to try and fly it.

I was restless inside, as though we were testing something other than the kite. Lying on the sofa for weeks, staring at our beautiful Christmas tree, I had been questioning my decision over and over. How could I do this to my family? How could I be so selfish? *My mother stayed,* I remember thinking to myself. And when I was much younger, she was one of the saddest, most guilt-ridden women I knew. I wanted to be happier than she had been.

The day to test the kite finally came, a clear, sunny day with a nice breeze. Together we took the kite back to the mountain. We watched it continue to rise and float in the air until all the string was used up. We ran with it as it leaped in the wind, flying like it was brand-new. A miracle!

We brought it down and carefully put it in the car. We would probably never fly it again, but I couldn't let go of something that had taught me such an eloquent lesson: I was sure from that day on that there are second chances in life for those who have the heart to reach for them.

INDIAN SUMMER

I mmersed in the heady anticipation of being independent for
the first time in my life, I prepared to live without my husband.
Angel nevertheless convinced me to undergo a six-month trial
separation before determining to leave him and the Foreign Service. He arranged for a brief tour with the State Department to
accommodate this.

Once again we jumped into the pond in front of us, this time
in the beautiful city of Rome. The embassy moved us into an
apartment a block away from the American School on the Cassia
del Norte. Angel came and went; his assignment was to travel
around Europe doing consulting work.

Haunted by the atmosphere in my house when I was a child,
I didn't want to repeat its cold silences. I was determined to get a
divorce as soon as we left Rome.

Slow down, Marilea. Take a breath, Angel seemed to be telling me in my sleep. But I didn't pay attention. I always barreled
straight ahead with my desires, often behaving rashly.

It was a beautiful balmy fall in Rome that year, and the sun
felt warm on my face as I took long walks up and down the Cassia
del Norte. The kids joined me often, and we found a favorite pizza
place that served white pizza, something we had never eaten in

the States. I can still taste the crust—completely different from American pizza.

The children took turns walking Oscar. Just as he had in Greece, Oscar provided them with a steadiness and unconditional love they all needed in those unsettling times.

Animals. School activities. Keeping busy. I was always there.

On the surface, the children were taking the separation in stride.

Except Annie.

RED FLAG

My eleven-year-old daughter was picked by a movie scout for a small role in a film that was being shot in Rome. He'd been hanging around the school campus and noticed her right away. She enjoyed it, but I worked hard to collect her paycheck.

I hunted down the production company and demanded the eight hundred dollars they owed her before we left the country. Seeing that I wasn't going to forget about it, the secretary nervously cut me a check just as the movers were packing them out.

"Here you go," she said, her eyes boring into me and my tenacity, "have a safe trip back to the States."

"Thanks." I grabbed the check and slammed the door as I left.

On the way home, I pigged out on pizza and gelato, hoping to walk off the calories. Rome was a tempting place to indulge my overeating compulsion. But I was about to get smacked in the face with Annie's brief run-in with anorexia nervosa, and the irony was unsettling.

My daughter spent every penny of that money on Jane Fonda's exercise tapes. No longer a gymnast, she turned her body into an obsession. Eating was the battleground where her internal struggles played out. I recognized that place only too well; it was like looking in a mirror. In her case, she all but stopped eating.

"Annie, your eggs are on the table. They'll get cold."

"No thanks, Mom. I'm not hungry," she responded, her voice listless.

That dialogue repeated itself at most meals, and I was so worried, seeing her slip into that familiar dark place. Some days her legs hurt so much she couldn't even walk to school.

I sat on her bed one morning, kneading the cramps out of her legs, wondering with every stroke if she would ever forgive me for taking her father away from her.

My heart ached for my daughter. It was clear how much she missed Angel.

Carter and Caroline stayed lost in their own thoughts, saying nothing about Annie's behavior—the same sort of poor communication and silence so reminiscent of growing up in my family.

The embassy doctor gave her vitamins and nothing more. He told her to eat her vegetables and never doubt how much her parents loved her. That spell of not eating appeared to resolve itself quickly after a few months. But it was the warning sign of something much more serious.

Annie was screaming, and Angel and I were too distracted by our own problems to pay closer attention.

Our time in Rome was Annie's first cry for help.

TRAINS
AND PLANES

The children and I came home from Italy in the cold winter of 1991. All of us, including our dear Oscar, went right to a hotel at Tysons Corner in northern Virginia and stayed there for a couple of weeks while we waited for our house to be vacant. Squeezing into my rental car, we drove to the nearest Giant supermarket for food and bought things we hadn't seen or eaten in almost four years: boxed cereals, chips, chocolate syrup, all the affordable processed foods that Americans take for granted but cost a lot in European markets.

Concealing my cravings at the checkout line, I decided to take us all to McDonald's for supper. I had two orders of fries, two Big Macs, and a large vanilla shake. We, except for Annie, were thrilled to be back in the land of fast food on every corner.

Our large hotel room was crowded with four people and a dog living in it. But when the kids had lapsed into a coma from all the sugar, I turned on the shower and purged in the bathroom. Oscar slept right through it too.

Finally, the moving company arrived with our household belongings—all that had been sitting in storage for the nine months since we left Greece, along with what we'd had with us in Rome—and we could move into our rented house. I couldn't believe how I managed all the coordination on my own with three kids and a dog.

"Marilea," my mother hollered out the front door on moving day, "I taped the directional signs on all the rooms so the movers know where to go with what! You can sit on the lawn and direct them from there."

"Thanks, Mom." I'd had to have surgery on my leg, and I beamed at her, grateful that she had come again to help me at a difficult time.

My reconciliation with my mother was an unexpected gift for us both, but by then I had been firmly in my addiction for decades. I already knew it would take more than my mother's acceptance of my divorce to free me of it.

I had a great deal of interior work to do. There were years of negative self-talk, self-loathing, and guilt that I needed to figure out and work through. I had my mother, and I would have so much more. Yet I didn't quite have myself. The pieces to the puzzle weren't fitting together comfortably.

I would discover in subsequent years the extent of my sobriety—or lack of it. Choosing self-care over self-abuse has never been a single light-bulb moment for me but rather an ongoing effort to educate and re-parent myself. And like many people with addictive personalities, I would find new and not particularly innovative ways to take the sting out of my pain.

When my mother was visiting us, she usually enjoyed a watered-down glass of wine in the living room as I fixed dinner. Before joining her with my own glass of wine, I would dawdle at my cutting board, preparing cheese and crackers while chugging wine right out of the bottle, cutting carrots and celery, then indulging in a few more swigs.

The peeling of an onion.

One layer at a time.

SPLIT

Angel sacrificed his next European post in Vienna and arranged to be reassigned to the United States. Determined to stay as close as possible, he found an apartment in Alexandria that June. One evening in July, he came over and had supper with all of us. I don't remember what we ate. I just remember the tears from a man who never, ever cried.

He addressed the children at the table as we were finishing our supper:

"Kids, your mother and I have decided to get a divorce," he started out, his voice cracking. I felt myself turn into a statue, fearful that if I didn't, I would bend right then and there and lose my resolve. I was afraid I would change my mind and stay in an unhappy marriage.

I froze, unable to look into their faces.

"I'm sure you know that we've been unhappy for a long time, and we feel it's best to end our marriage now. But I've taken a job here in Washington and will be living in an apartment close by in Alexandria. You know I love you and will see you whenever you want."

The speech was before his fourteen-year-old son, the boy whose games he always went to—with a book, of course. Before his twelve-year-old daughter, the daughter he'd watched being

200

born, the one he would be closest to. Before his ten-year-old baby, the one named for his aunt and grandmother.

I remember the five of us sitting around the dinner table, like a still shot in a camera. As with many other painful experiences in my life, I don't have a clear memory of what happened at the meal. Like, for example, how my children reacted. Or what I said, if anything.

I've simply blacked it out.

What is clear in my memory is that man sitting at the head of a table that would cease to be his. He had spent nearly two years hoping to save our marriage for all the best reasons. And now he was admitting defeat, tearfully telling his children that our family was irretrievably broken.

Angel went right home after dinner. The children retreated to their rooms. A bottle of brandy under my bedside table was my new evening companion. Feeling its burn as it went into my stomach helped me get to sleep at night.

I felt broken in half by the weight of my life and my choices.

Part Three

WAKING UP

Oh, the places you'll go! There is fun to be done!
There are points to be scored. There are games
to be won. And the magical things you can do with that
ball will make you the winning-est winner of all.

—Dr. Seuss, *Oh, the Places You'll Go!* [14]

NICHE

I'm nobody! Who are you?
Are you nobody, too?

—Emily Dickinson[15]

That spring after returning from Rome, I wasted no time beginning my job search. My first paycheck came from teaching adult education at night.

It took thirty minutes for me to drive from my house to Herndon, Virginia. I spent nearly every weeknight teaching English to newly arrived Hispanics, many of whom fought "coyotes" in the Mexican desert or made it across the Rio Grande in a floating tire, dodging bullets. Strangely, I identified with them. I knew what it felt like to bang on a locked door.

A dozen years later, I wrote in my graduate school journal, "10/15/2003: I realize now why I love teaching immigrants: the isolated child in me identifies with the foreign students. We're all outsiders! What a light-bulb moment that was for me!"

SINGLE MOM

A ngel and I divorced amicably. We went through mediation and agreed on the terms of financial support. He was more than generous. We were awarded joint custody, and our lawyer assumed that the children would divide their time between us.

But it didn't work out that way. Though he was always pleasant toward me, Angel was angry about the divorce. And he left me largely on my own to raise our children. We did not share custody; except for a ski trip to Italy to visit their dad when he was working in Rome, our kids lived with me virtually all the time. There were no regular weekends with Dad, summers with Dad, holidays with Dad. What he did on a regular basis was come over to our house every Sunday for dinner. He was a great cook, and the children looked forward to that.

Soon after we were divorced in 1992, Annie fell into a depression that I don't believe she's ever come out of. We were quick to find a therapist for her to see every week, and she seemed to get better. So much so that when Angel was awarded a stellar post in Rome as deputy chief of mission to the Vatican, he felt sure that she would be okay if he left the country. So he accepted the assignment in 1994, and had he stayed there, it might have moved him farther up the ladder in the State Department. He might even have achieved his dream of becoming an ambassador one day. But his career trajectory ended with a tearful phone call from Annie in 1995:

"Dad, come home. I need you."

That was all it took.

The kids needed their father in their life as well as me. They must have felt that when he gave up on me, he gave up on them too. And they must have felt that I did as well. I was busy working full-time and going to graduate school in order to keep my job, often not at home to supervise the children. Nor was I always emotionally present for them, still too distracted with my own problems.

Feeling terribly guilty about the breakup of my family, I thought I deserved the stress that went with full custody of three teenagers. I should have put all those feelings aside, though, and considered what would be best for our children. They needed the balance that two parents could have provided. I needed it.

I wrote in my journal in the summer of 1991:

I've chosen to be independent from Angel. I made the choice one and a half years ago. And six months ago, by leaving him and bringing the children home to DC, I began my journey. At first, back in February, I was flying high on a heady sense of power, feeling strong to pack up and come here on my own. But I was completely self-absorbed in my own struggle to build an identity of my own, apart from Angel.

Staying on this path without the love and support of my husband is difficult. It's the day-to-day things that wear down my reserves. I have to do everything myself, from dishes to home repairs to being the major parent for my kids. It takes up so much of my energy.

And now that we're separated, where is he? How could I think that I could break up my family and just smoothly sail out into the work world without any complications? I was dreaming, and now I'm waking up and seeing more realistically the consequences of my decision to live independently.

A DAY
IN THE LIFE

My diary entry from February of 1992:

> Alarm goes off at 5:30, leaving an extra half hour to fix cereal for the kids. Annie and Caroline catch the bus for middle school and Carter, a block away from the high school, whenever, I don't know exactly. I'll be on my way to my new job teaching high school at 6:30 before they finish breakfast. Miraculously, they always manage to make it to school without a hitch.
>
> At school my last bell rings at 2:10, and I'll be in my car at 2:15. Occasionally my supervisor is annoyed when I miss a number of after-school meetings, but I want to be there when the kids get home. Opening the front door, I hear Jane Fonda huffing through her routine. Annie at thirteen looks cute in her leg warmers.
>
> "One hour—and then hit the books, please."
>
> I go to my room and collapse on my bed. How can I do this: prepare for five classes tomorrow and race out to Herndon to teach adult education? But first, dinner: grilled cheese sandwiches that I don't know if they'll eat. Once again my means of survival eclipses any

supervision of my kids. But they seem to be doing a great job of raising themselves.

I run out to my class at 6:00 and sleepwalk through adult English as a Second Language that I am teaching, much of the time, in Spanish to twenty El Salvadorians. My methods are awful but it's a paycheck, and they love it that I speak their language.

Dragging myself through the front door, I hear Annie and Carter screaming over the TV.

"Is this what I have to come home to after a hard day at work?" I ask.

"Mom, Carter kicked me right in the gut. It hurts."

"She kept changing the channel, Mom. Tonight is my night to choose."

"Work it out yourselves, you two. Or better yet, time for bed."

I was only just beginning to see the price I paid for working in my chosen career. The guilt from breaking up my family wore away at me.

Wolfing down all the leftover grilled cheese sandwiches, I added some cookies and a quart of ice cream. Two cups of tea loosened it up in my stomach, and it came back up into the toilet pretty easily. I fell into bed, hating myself for giving in to this addiction and wishing I could stop. I was so tired of it.

But there was a new part of me that was slowly being born. I was determined to feed another hunger that had lingered since Nicaragua. Even through all the exhaustion, regret, and tears, I was coming alive in my classroom.

So I kept going.

LISTEN!

Teaching is mostly listening,
and learning is mostly telling.

—Deborah Meier[16]

Rehearsing a scene from *West Side Story* with my advanced ESL class, I was enjoying the kids play-acting in familiar territory.

"I like to be in America, okay by me in America . . ." They were chanting the lyrics from the musical.

"Cut! Cut!" I shouted to Alia, my student from Pakistan, seeing her discomfort with the lines.

"Alia, don't worry about pronunciation. The characters are from Puerto Rico, remember, and they roll their *r*'s, but do whatever is easy for you."

"Thanks, miss. I'm embarrassed playing Anita. I forget the lines, and I don't have a Spanish accent."

"But you have a lovely Arabic accent, Alia, and don't you ever lose it. You're beautiful just the way you are!"

"Thanks, miss."

Alia went back to her role aware, right then, that it was just a role.

"And I like your Anita," I added, winking.

She relaxed and started having fun, getting her confidence back.

Alia graduated three years later. I received a holiday card from her five years after her graduation when I was still living in Virginia.

"I'm married with two kids, miss, and I'm very happy."

How wonderful that in helping a disenfranchised population to find its voice, I became increasingly aware of my own.

"Thank you, Gretchen," I would say to my advisor twelve years later in graduate school, "thank you for being such a good listener."

THREES

There's a Greek song that says after leaving Greece one must return *"treis forés"* (three times) for good luck.

Three years after we left Greece, I went back during my summer vacation and enjoyed the first of three return visits with my old friend Eleni and her husband, Nondas.

Eleni hates the strong northern winds, the *meltemi*, that batter the Mediterranean during the summer months. She avoids leaving the peninsula of Athens and going to the Greek islands during August when everyone else descends upon them like locusts.

Only a Greek could find the islands unpleasant—all six thousand of them, two hundred inhabited, so exotic and intoxicating, drawing millions of tourists every year. But my good friend made a concession for me during my visit that year, and together with her husband we took the ferry to Sifnos for a long weekend.

Sifnos lies in the Cyclades, one of several groups of Greek islands, this one south of Athens in the heart of the Greek Mediterranean. We chose that particular island because Nondas has family there, family who would occupy him while Eleni and I spent our days together.

My friend and I lay on the jagged rocks just close enough to the surf to refresh ourselves if the heat became oppressive. The continual breeze and the cool salt spray were delightful. The water was so clear that my eyes could see down to the ocean floor, and I dove in.

But then with the turbulence of my splash, the transparency was lost, and like a fortune-teller out of a job, I couldn't see what was coming next.

I used to think that if I had known what life had in store for me, I would have done things differently. But I don't believe that now. No one has a crystal ball, and God help me if I had.

Exploring the rocks underwater, I was startled by an octopus nestled there and quickly scampered back onto our perch. Eleni was napping, so I let my mind wander. I was remembering dancing with her at her home during the carnival celebrations— Apokries, which are like the Dionysian revels they recall—night after night in my costume and mask, a respite from the reality that had been unfolding in my house just up the road from hers: the beginning of my unmasking, which would go on for many more years, layers being peeled away—with life happening in between.

OUT OF
THE BLUE

The ink wasn't dry on my divorce when Gene swept into my life. The last thing I needed was another man at that time. But some of the best things come to us when we least expect them. That's how it was with Angel. Oh, what a charmer he was! Juan from San Juan had just dumped me, and I was sick of men at Harvard. But ever the diplomat, Angel was convinced that a life with me would be a rewarding adventure. And, despite my personal struggles, it was.

Now I had two children in high school, and Caroline was still in middle school. She came down with tonsillitis and needed to have her tonsils removed, which meant an overnight in the hospital. I was there in the morning when she woke up. She had a morphine drip and a brutal sore throat. I took her home and mothered her before going back to work two days later.

The day before Caroline's surgery, I was busy leaving lesson plans in my classroom for the substitute. I hated being absent from my students and usually left a pile of easy work for them. Sometimes I left a movie, but I preferred they do something interactive.

A handsome, tall fellow walked by my room.

"I don't see a number out here. Is this 23D?" he called out, looking at me, not the door.

"Yes, it is. Can I help you?"

"Are you Mrs. Rabasa? I'm scheduled to sub for you tomorrow."

"Yes, my name's Marilea. And you are?"

"Gene. Gene Dunne," he answered, coming in and offering to shake my hand.

Wow, what a classy guy, I was thinking, instantly attracted to him. *But Caroline needs me at home.*

"I've really gotta run. I have a sick child at home. But here's my number," I offered, scribbling my phone number on a piece of paper. "Call me if you have any questions."

"Sure, thanks," he said, ripping a piece of paper out of the notebook he was carrying. "Here's mine too."

"Nice to meet you. And good luck tomorrow." We left the classroom, and I locked my door and ran off, leaving him standing there.

Well, my phone didn't start ringing. But there was something about him that drew me in. And I wanted to find out what it was.

I called him once or twice to chat. When I asked him how he enjoyed teaching my classes, he sounded mildly annoyed.

"Well, every class asked me when you were coming back, so either I was doing my job badly or you were doing it well. Either way, I was glad to start another assignment after yours."

It turned out that we both loved opera. I used to listen to the Met with my mother on Saturday afternoons, and Gene was moonlighting as a telemarketer at the Washington National Opera. I took the initiative by inviting him to a performance of *Turandot* at George Mason University, picking him up and dropping him off in the pouring rain—but there was no kiss goodnight.

A couple of weeks later, he took me to see Donizetti's *Anna Bolena* with his daughter. She was adorable, and it was nice meeting her.

He didn't appear all that interested, though, and I was feeling frustrated. I learned later that Gene had been coming off a long-term relationship and was in no hurry to fall in love again. Neither was I, or so I thought.

One Sunday afternoon in December, not my favorite month of the year, an increasingly familiar numbing agent, my brandy bottle, looked inviting. Going outside after an ice storm to shovel the driveway, I slipped, fell on the ice, and broke my ankle.

We did wish each other Merry Christmas over the phone. I wasn't going anywhere in my cast. But he invited me to another opera the following month. Encouraged and feeling buoyant, I looked forward to our date.

The year ahead held much promise for both of us. As we enjoyed *The Dream of Valentino* at the Kennedy Center, I was sitting on his lap before the end of the show. We were entirely swept away with each other. We weren't afraid to offend the patrons sitting near us. In fact, after we all applauded the performers, a few of the audience members applauded us as we pulled our overheated and embarrassed selves together and stumbled, me hobbling in my cast, out the door to the parking garage.

That night was a memorable one.

STILL HIDING

G ene was offered a contract in the same school district as me a couple of years after we met in my classroom. Our lives happily revolved around each other, the five children we had between us, and our jobs. We delighted in being colleagues in the same county, bumping into each other at meetings, stealing kisses around corners, and simply enjoying the proximity of our jobs.

We saved time by living and working near each other. And time was what we were catching up on: there we were in midlife, starting over. We didn't want to waste a minute.

Raising three teenagers largely on my own was stressful, and Gene's presence in my life was an unexpected blessing that elevated me above the day-to-day responsibilities of running a large house, managing single motherhood, going to work, and taking graduate school courses. But just as I had hidden so much of my self-destructive behavior from Angel throughout our relationship, I did the same with Gene during the early years of our partnership, and for the same reasons. I was afraid he would lose interest in me, that he would think he was taking on more than he could handle.

Though the binge-purge cycle occurred with far less frequency, I still indulged my food addiction on occasion, usually over the holidays, and I was too ashamed to allow Gene to peek into that window. That part of me was closed off from him and, at that point in my life, from everyone else. How well, then, did he know me? If I felt disconnected from people, it was my own doing. Intimacy was lacking in a majority of my relationships throughout my life as I continued to wear masks to cover up my addictions. This certainly was the reason for much of my loneliness and isolation. It would take several more years for me to take the risks necessary to have healthier relationships.

Gene's children were close in age to mine. Bridget, his daughter, was a budding young actor, and we enjoyed going to all her performances. Patrick was three years older than his sister and was showing an interest in film production. Both of Gene's children lived with their mother, but they saw him regularly.

All my children worked at jobs after school, had their own cars, and pitched in to pay their own expenses—compensating, no doubt, for my emotional distance. Carter, in particular, stepped up, becoming "the man of the house" in his father's absence, not uncommon in single-parent families. This encouraged a false sense of security in me, and not a little complacency. I didn't see the burden it placed on him. With three teenagers reeling from divorce, I should have been more vigilant.

Little had changed from when they were preschoolers; between my job, grad school, my new relationship with Gene, and my ever-present addictions, they were not in the forefront of my life as they should have been. I was still broken on the inside, trying to appear competent and successful while pushing my demons away. It was around this time, in my mid-forties, that instead of compulsive overeating on a regular basis I began drinking alcoholically with more frequency. I'd grown tired of the binge-purge cycle of overeating; like many addictions, it had become a burden I wanted to be free of as I took on a new one.

Picking a recovering alcoholic for a partner was no accident. Though I was a closet drinker at first, I began drinking in front of Gene, sometimes at the end of the day to unwind, other times with a nice steak, and when Caroline dyed her hair green.

I couldn't face it at the time, but I was certainly using alcohol in excess—just as I had used food—to withstand the inevitable pressures of living.

"Hey, babe, the bottle's nearly empty," Gene wryly observed as we sat down to the prime rib he had prepared for us. "Can I pour us some water to drink with dinner?" It was unlike him to be critical, and he knew better than to interfere with an addict's behavior.

"Relax, Gene, we're not going anywhere afterward." I bristled at my exposure. Overindulgence on my part was infrequent—both a good thing and a bad thing: good because the potential consequences were fewer in number; bad because my disease would progress stealthily but reliably over the course of the next twenty-six years.

Alcoholism is a patient taskmaster.

Gene saw what I was doing, but he knew better than to press his concerns. Sometimes, if I couldn't indulge my addiction when I wanted to, I could get downright nasty.

After his divorce several years earlier, Gene had taken up canoeing with his best friend, Jack, and I proved to be a quick study. On one of our canoe trips to Canada, Jack brought his own version of cocktail hour.

He had a collapsible glass that he poured, I'm not kidding, about a quarter of an ounce of bourbon into. He sat there at the end of a demanding day of paddling, needing to unwind with the rest of us. Gene wasn't tempted; he had been sober for a decade by then. He and I smoked unfiltered Camels.

But I was (tempted). My thoughts around alcohol revealed my wish to get plastered more and more. Seeing him there with his glass in hand, I wished I'd planned better and brought my own cocktail hour—that I were joining him with a full glass of vodka to unwind.

Staring at Jack and his bourbon across the campfire, my eyes reflecting the flames in front of us, I squirmed with envy and frustration, and howled under my breath, *Jack, how is that teeny amount of bourbon gonna do anything for you?*

MY SECOND WIND

G ene tried to step up and win the affection of my children. After we bought the first of our three canoes together, Annie asked to go with us to Violette's Lock on the Maryland side of the Potomac River. We should have bought a third paddle for her, as she lay like a princess on the floor in the middle of the boat. Gene missed a valuable opportunity to introduce her to paddling.

"How'd you like canoeing, Annie?" Gene asked her when we got home. "Wouldn't it be fun to go out again?"

"Maybe," she answered without much enthusiasm.

"Well, I'm glad you came, Annie," I piped in. "Maybe if we get you a paddle, you'll be more engaged and like it better."

"Yeah, maybe."

Gene and I lived in a world apart from my teenage children, it seemed. Though I was familiar with Puccini operas from listening to them with my mother, Gene not only knew opera but also sang as a bass one year in the chorus of *Carmen* and *Faust* at the National Lyric Opera, a small local company in the District of Columbia. At his house not far from mine, he tutored me by poring over the librettos to every opera he took me to, and his part-time job gave him access to dress rehearsals of all of the Washington Opera performances. Opera became a big part of our lives, an attraction that would point us to Santa Fe, home of a world-class opera, years later.

My children weren't interested in opera, nor did they want Gene and me to teach them how to paddle. They kept quiet and busy but showed little interest in bonding with my new boyfriend.

The kids did well enough in school, rarely got into any kind of trouble, and chose to pursue college. Annie was faithfully seeing her therapist, dealing with her depression. Life had certainly knocked them around some going through divorce and missing a closer connection with their father. But I did a lot of rationalizing: *Things could be so much worse! I love my job, I love my kids, I love Gene. Ain't life grand?* Clyde Barrow, in *Bonnie and Clyde*, crowed to his brother Buck as they faced one calamity after another, "Ain't life grand?"

Oh, what teachers we are to our children! I was highly invested in teaching my students in high school, while I let my own children learn plenty of unintended lessons on the home front.

So distracted by the whirlwind of our happy lives, Gene and I didn't see what was hiding in plain sight right in front of us.

Like my mother before me, I kept up appearances, and like my old self, I felt ashamed of my addictions. And I wasn't paying close attention to my children.

LOBSTER DINNER

Summers became our escape together. A sitter stayed in the house for two weeks so Gene and I could take off and see the country. Many of our trips involved backpacking and camping in one of the national parks. Gene had been to several of them and was eager to show me the beauty of our country. But before we took any of our trips, we always went to Massachusetts to see my mother, still living independently in her condominium. She was anxious to visit with me after the long school year.

Gene and I drove up to see her one summer just before one of our canoeing trips. We brought the canoe and planned to paddle around the marshes nearby.

Mother looked forward to our visits. She always loved to entertain in style, so she got lobsters for dinner one night, one of Gene's favorite treats in New England. He drove to the lobster pound to buy them, just as my father had done every Friday night during the summer. In the meantime, I started the water boiling in the big lobster kettle and dug through her kitchen drawers looking for the tools and bibs she rarely used. My eyes spotted the corkscrew, and I took it out as well.

"Marilea, there's a bottle of white wine in the fridge," Mother called out from the living room as though she were reading my mind. "Just a half a glass for me, then dilute it with water."

"Sure, Mom. I'll join you." I smiled, remembering how she avoided getting high from alcohol. I was relieved that someone had already opened the bottle, as I'd never had much luck with corkscrews and I have the scar to prove it. I drank a glass like it was water before joining her with a second in the living room. More and more, alcohol was reeling me in like a fish on a line. It was becoming a regular attempt to push the angry voices out of my head:

"Marilea, look at yourself!" Mom squeezed my roomy hips from behind as we stood in front of the hall mirror. "What are we going to do about this?"

"Put your shoes on! You've got the ugliest feet I've ever seen," Dad growled through one too many gin and tonics.

"You know I could have killed you here tonight." Samuel sneered at me from his woods home in Bermuda.

Voices from the past and a troubled adolescence. But they weren't in the past now; they were still taking up space in my head. I would need to let go of the fears I'd experienced within my family and elsewhere—make peace with all that had happened before. Until I did that, it would be difficult to move on.

The water was ready by the time Gene came in with the live lobsters. I had to leave the room when he plopped them to their hopefully instant death. I had always hated watching my father do the same thing.

That was the ritual whenever Gene and I came to visit. Mother looked forward to it because it brought Daddy back. She missed him more and more even though their marriage had not been a happy one. Alcoholism stole so much from her. More than once she told me that she wished she had treated him with more kindness. Though he had died in 1985, I could still see him like a ghost sitting at the head of the table eating what was also his favorite meal, slobbering it all over himself until Mother, disgusted by his sloppiness, could get a bib around his neck. He devoured not only the meat of the lobster but all the green stuff, too, the tomalley—a delicacy, he called it!

Mother didn't even like to eat lobster—she had a piece of sole—but she got them for us because she knew how much of a treat it would be for Gene. We spent what seemed like hours picking each of those crustaceans apart.

First was the easy part: cracking the tail open, pulling the meat out, and gobbling that up, really a meal in itself. In restaurants they charge you a lot just for the tail. Then came the next easiest part, the claws; that was my favorite. I liked the smooth texture of the meat—smooth but not slimy—with some white creamy covering on the outside. I cracked open each claw and used the little fork to pull the meat out. The meat separated in the right claw, and I had to crack it again to get it all—annoying. It's better when it all sort of glides out in one piece.

Mom had to keep melting butter—the real thing, not oleo—because Gene had two whole lobsters, and he liked to dip the meat in it. Being so weight conscious, I avoided the butter. But it wasn't necessary; the distinctive flavor sufficed.

Then came the part of the meal we lingered over while Gene and I talked to Mom about our teaching careers. We broke open the legs, pulled out the meat with our little forks, and what we couldn't pull out we sucked out ravenously. It reminded me of my housekeeper Isabel in Ecuador who, I swear, acted like she hadn't had a chicken in her whole life the way she sucked the marrow out of every single bone, rolling her eyes in ecstasy long after the meat was gone.

Mom was fascinated with our adventures in the classroom.

She had always wanted to have a career in teaching, and she enjoyed living out her dream vicariously through us.

"Gene, what is the difference between your job and Marilea's? You're both English teachers, right?"

"Yes, Peg, but Marilea teaches English as a Second Language to immigrants. And I teach regular English to American kids."

Gene was realizing that my eighty-eight-year-old mother was still living in the cultural bubble of that upper-class New England town. She didn't see what the nation's capital and other parts of the United States saw: planeloads of refugees from war-torn countries arriving in America, just hoping to be granted asylum and stay alive.

That was the circumstance of a few of my students, but not all of them. Most had come to find work and get a better education.

"Mom, do I need to remind you that Angel and I lived in Nicaragua and Ecuador? Many of those kids left their countries behind to find a better life in our country. And it's my job to teach them English."

"Oh, of course. Well, maybe you understand them a little since you lived in their country."

"More than you know, Mom," I said, smiling at the irony of how much I identified as an outsider.

It was getting late, and we needed to go to bed. While Gene was upstairs taking a shower, Mom and I chatted as we cleaned up the kitchen.

"I'm so glad you're with Gene." My once-ambitious mother who would have loved for me to run off with an Arabian prince had stopped needing me to live out her fantasies of wealth and power.

She was accepting and appreciative of the man I had chosen to love after my divorce. I always thought Mother enjoyed Gene because he was the man my father might have become if he'd stopped drinking for good. Like my dad, he loved all kinds of music—especially jazz and Louis Armstrong—was a vocalist, a talented writer and poet, and a self-made man who, at one point, enjoyed working for himself, and had a killer sense of humor. And he was a recovering alcoholic.

If the two of them had only met! Dad died too young from the disease. And Gene, blessedly, hasn't had a drink in over thirty years. I've never known him when he was drinking. My partner of twenty-six years goes to recovery meetings every day.

It's been a slow wheel, my journey to wellness. Recovery has opened new doors for me—one called trust and the other called faith. It has taken me to a new level of honesty with Gene, and though I was openly drinking at that point, what a revelation to uncover a worrisome habit and find my loving partner still there in front of me.

We ground and support each other. He's always been my best friend—even when we're mad at each other.

Many times while paddling on the Canadian lakes, he told me to look for a take-out for the canoe.

"Well, how do I know what a take-out looks like, Gene?" I groaned, frustrated that he assumed I would know. "I'm just looking at trees all around the shore."

"Honey, look for a spot that's a little wider, an opening."

"An opening? That opening over there?" I pointed across the lake to the right. "At the end of the waterfall?"

"No, Marilea, that's not a good place to take out our boat." Always ultra-sensitive, I felt he was patronizing the hell out of me.

"You wanna get all wet?" he joked.

Gentle and fun, Gene always lifts me up when I'm down, a steady angel beneath my fragile wings.

RIPTIDE

In 1998 I made my second trip back to Greece as I had promised Eleni. By then my friends had bought a summer home in Volos, two hundred kilometers north of Athens on a windswept peninsula jutting out into the Aegean Sea. Coming from the humidity of Virginia, I reveled once again in the dry heat in Greece—and the quality of light, unique in its clarity and the reason why so many artists flock there.

After resting a day from my long flight, we drove to Volos. Eleni feared I'd be disappointed, staying in that provincial city instead of hopping on the ferry to one of the Sporades, a group of picturesque islands nearby. But I had been to many of the Greek islands, and it mattered little to me where I was with her. She and I have shared an attraction, a connection, a wonder about each other that has simply never gone away over these thirty years. When we are together, our glass is full.

One day, six of us piled into Nondas's car to escape the sizzling city heat. It was a long ride to the northern coast on the Pelion Peninsula, but the trip was worth it. The beach at Agios Ioannis and its surf were magnificent. Long, lazy Greek lunches take place at tables with many friends, big chunks of fish, seasonal vegetables slathered in olive oil, fresh bread, and *krasí*—always plenty of *krasí*, a dreadful white wine that tastes a little like turpentine.

Or ouzo, drunk straight or made into a murky white drink with water. I loved the sweet anise-flavored liqueur and drank it straight without diluting it. Lunch on this day was no different, involving many courses of food, cigarettes, wine, and stimulating conversation. It was a long, luxurious, three-hour affair followed by a much-needed nap. The way Greeks live, and not just in the summertime, is a delicious respite from our American rat race.

For some reason I wanted to keep a clear head and drank water with lunch; Eleni and I didn't nap that day. All the men were sleeping soundly in the beach house while we decided to brave the strong waves. There was a powerful undertow where we were, and I remembered from my summers swimming at Nauset Beach on Cape Cod how dangerous an undertow could be. I started falling into my familiar cave of fear. But Eleni grabbed my hand.

She dragged me along, and we ran toward the glorious surf pounding in front of us.

"Oh no!" I shrieked, trying to stop her. "Wait for it to break. We'll drown!"

Who was I kidding? I wasn't afraid of the big water. I was a child again. And Eleni was eight years old with me, laughing and telling me not to be afraid.

Love—how it pulls at me in my sleep. How it straightens my spine and puts energy in my stride to propel me forward.

DAMAGES

"Dear Eleni," I wrote to my friend after I returned from Greece. "I am so sad that I'm not closer to my girls. Caroline wants nothing to do with me, and Annie plays along by the rules, but I know there are things she's hiding from me. I don't know how to get her to trust me. I'll sit on her bed in her darkened room and plead with her to open up to me. But she just stares into space or tells me she can only talk to her therapist. So I leave her alone. What can I do? I feel like I'm losing them both."

"Marilea, just keep talking to them," she advised in her response. "Never stop trying to get inside their heads and communicate with them. I know it's frustrating. But I know how much you love them, and though they seem unresponsive, they know it too."

Every year I'd made a tremendous effort on Christmas: the beautiful Christmas tree, glistening with ornaments we'd picked up from around the world; the white lights in every window calling attention to our house; roast beef and Yorkshire pudding, the way my mother had always prepared it.

On Christmas morning of 1999, I received a tearful call from Caroline somewhere in the city. Her car totaled, she was in need of help. So I ran out the door to rescue her and her car, giving Carter and Annie instructions on how to cook the roast. I sat around in my car for at least six hours waiting for the tow truck; that Christmas morning, there were many drunken accidents in need of a cleanup. Reading magazines to pass the time, I fumed at my daughter for not being there in my place. She was sleeping soundly at her friend's house while I cleaned up after her.

I remember coming home at five in the afternoon, exhausted, to silence and a burned roast. Collapsing at the kitchen table in a joyless house, empty and flat like an airless balloon, I poured too much vodka into a tumbler, trying to drown the disappointment and guilt that were gripping me. The lights on our Christmas tree dimmed and, as if on cue, went out in several places.

This was not the first nor would it be the last Christmas when my children were telling me, without telling me, that they longed for Christmas of another sort—one where Mom and Dad still lived together and loved each other. Gene rented a house not too far away, and Angel had remarried a few years before. They had lost all hope of their parents' reconciliation.

Holidays must have been brutal for them.

MY DAUGHTER/
MYSELF

The following summer, Oscar developed such serious health problems that we had to put him down. In July, Angel came over to say goodbye to him. Then Carter and I walked him to the vet and held him down while he received his injection. Annie couldn't bear to be there. As we were sobbing over his dying body, unable to leave, the aide gently suggested that we needed to let go of him. We left the building, and Carter and I held on to each other all the way home. Annie stayed in her room, and I tried, unsuccessfully, to reach her.

"Annie," I said, knocking on her door, "please let me in. I know how you feel. We're all sad to lose Oscar. I just want to hug you and tell you it'll be okay. Please don't isolate yourself like this. Come out and get something to eat with me and Carter."

"Mom, I couldn't eat a thing right now. I just want to go to sleep. I'll see you in the morning."

I couldn't eat anything either. We were both stunned by the absence of our much-beloved dog, and, not surprisingly, we lost our appetites. Even bulimics can stop eating, at least for a while, when they're sad.

Another letting go served to uproot us as Angel and I sold our large house a month later. We all seemed to scatter like the four winds afterward. Caroline had moved to California, and Carter was living with a friend in DC. I found a condominium near my high school, and Annie moved into a friend's apartment.

Her first year of living independently seemed uneventful at first. Frequently visiting her in the apartment she shared, I took her furniture from her old bedroom so she would feel at home in her new digs. But there were signs that she was changing. She had never had many boyfriends in high school. Then one Sunday morning I arrived to find a friend of hers on the sofa, clearly feeling at home. Later I learned he was a bartender at a watering hole and drug hot spot in Adams Morgan. Well, she was on her own. And by now she was twenty-one; I didn't have much leverage.

In the spring, though two courses short of her graduation requirements at George Mason University, Annie was allowed to walk with her class, cap and gown and all.

Angel, his wife, and I all dressed up for our second child's college graduation in the spring of 2001, and we all viewed this ceremony as a symbol of hope that Annie was willing and anxious to embrace her adulthood and take on more responsibilities, like other young people.

"Hey, Mom, I want you to meet my friend Shelly. She got me through statistics sophomore year," Annie told me.

"Hi, Shelly, nice to meet you. Thanks for helping Annie. Is your family here today?"

"No. They had to work. No big deal for them anyway."

"Oh. Well, I think it's a big deal, so congratulations from me! It was nice to meet you, Shelly, and good luck."

Annie's graduation distracted us from being curious about what she was doing in the evenings. Again, she went to a lot of trouble to cover up behavior that she knew would alarm us and might threaten an intervention.

Just like her mother.

At the end of the summer, she asked if she could move into my basement. Her roommate was buying a condo, she said, and their lease was up anyway. Later on, when I watched in horror as the tragedy unfolded in my own house, I wondered about the truth of that. I thought maybe the roommate saw where Annie was going and asked her to leave. No matter. She was in my house now.

The circle was about to close.

Then came a shocking discovery—a bowl of homemade methamphetamine on top of my dryer! I had been wondering about the stuff she'd left in my basement laundry room. After reading the label—"muriatic acid"—I looked it up on my computer. *So that's what she used it for!*

I moved the bowl upstairs to the kitchen and put it next to the sink, where recessed lighting bore down on it. She couldn't miss it when she came in the front door. I thought I'd be ready for the confrontation.

At four thirty in the morning, she exploded into my bedroom while Gene and I were sleeping. I'm glad he was with me that night.

"How dare you mess with my things downstairs! Don't you ever touch my stuff again, you fucking bitch!" she roared. I thought I was dreaming when I saw her there, animal-like, with wild, bloodshot eyes.

Gene held on to me as I sobbed into my pillow. "Oh God, this isn't happening, Gene, please tell me this isn't happening!"

A half hour later, pulling myself together, I went downstairs to make coffee. I still had to go to work.

Annie stomped upstairs from the basement with a garbage bag full of her clothes and brushed by me without a word or a look. She slammed the door behind her. I ran to the kitchen window and saw her get into her car.

My daughter went from crystal meth to cocaine to heroin as though it were a smorgasbord of terrible choices. Despite four rehabs and a lot of family love, her addictive disease continued. There were periods of remission, but they were short-lived. My daughter lived in one pigsty after another, her boyfriends all drug addicts. I would spend a decade trying to reconcile two feelings: complete hatred for the stranger who was living in my daughter's body and total surrender to my love for her.

Because of our superficial differences, I didn't realize right away how alike we were.

We've both suffered from depression since we were young. The adults in our lives didn't always acknowledge our screams. We turned to using substances for relief: food, cigarettes, and drugs. I added alcohol to my list, but I'm not aware that she ever drank alcoholically. My daughter moved on to heroin.

At least I cleaned up well.

Though Annie was no longer living with me at that point, I tried to continue embracing her, accepting her, so she'd know she was still loved. But I couldn't yet distinguish between helping and enabling.

I did unwise, misguided things: I gave her money; I paid her debts; I shielded her from jail when she broke the law.

"Are you sure you don't want us to contact the authorities about this, Mrs. Rabasa?" the rep asked me when she stole my identity to get a credit card.

"Oh no," I said, terrified of her going to jail, "I'll handle it."

And I did, badly.

This was enabling at its worst. Since I was convinced her addiction came from me, that guilt crippled me and my judgment.

Placing a safety net beneath her only served to ease my anxiety. It did nothing to teach her the consequences of her behavior. I kept getting in her way.

It felt like I was in the twilight zone whenever I visited her. My daughter was buried somewhere deep inside, but the addict was in charge. One body, split down the middle: the Annalise I knew, and a hard-core drug addict. A surreal nightmare.

Her apartment smelled of incense and dirty laundry. The soles of her shoes flopped until she could get some duct tape around them. She didn't offer me anything to eat because there was no food in the refrigerator.

Nothing.

Twice while I was there, she ran to the bathroom to vomit.

Heroin. Dope sick.

Annie was hijacked by a cruel disease—cruel because it robs you of yourself while you're still alive. While destroying your mind, it keeps your body alive long enough to do a lot of damage before it actually kills you. For many drug addicts, it's an agonizingly slow death.

It was like watching a movie of my life in reverse, erasing all the good fortune that had brought me to where I was, leaving only the pain and ugliness—and hopelessness—of a wasted life. How I might have ended up.

For better or worse, my life had been unfolding as many do with addictive personalities. But to watch the same disease taking over the life of my child—to see that mirror up close in front of me—was threatening to be my undoing.

Trying to hold it together, I was imploding. Like all addicts and families of addicts, survival can be reached from many places, but often from the bottom.

Mine was waiting for me.

TWO-STEPPING
THE TWELVE STEP

"Marilea, why don't you try a recovery meeting?" my counselor gently advised me. She had heard me moan week after week about Annie turning into a monster I didn't recognize anymore. It was terrifying; sleep eluded me.

"Oh no, that's not for me," I responded, echoing my mother from thirty years before when my sister tried to get her to do the same thing.

"Well, I think it will help you to be around people going through the same thing."

After thinking about it for a few weeks, though, I took her advice and started going to a meeting on Saturday mornings. Gene also felt it was a good idea.

And so began a long period of faithfully going to twelve-step meetings but essentially paying lip service much of the time, particularly to the first three steps, because I was nothing if not the biggest control freak around.

Step One: Admit my powerlessness? Never! I brought her into the world. It was my job to protect and save her.

Step Two: Believe that God could restore me to sanity? What's insane about trying to save my child?

Step Three: Turn my will over to God? No way! I had to stay in control.

As a child, I took care of my own needs. I'd asked for company, hollered for attention, hoped for forgiveness, but I was often ignored. So I became compulsively self-reliant: CSR, I humorously say at meetings. And much of that self-reliance, attempting to appear competent, looked like arrogance.

It took me a long time before I found the humility to get a sponsor. Part of me didn't want to ask for help; an even bigger part thought I didn't need help. It was Annie, I argued, who needed help.

Humility, I discovered, was a tremendous leveler, and it would bring me closer to what I'd been missing my whole life: being part of a community of equals.

But without being honest with myself and others, I remained isolated on the outside, looking in.

FEAR

G azing at my masks hanging on the wall—one from Honduras, one from the Amazon, and the one I made while earning my master of arts in teaching—I wonder why I'd collected and saved them all. What was my fascination with face masks?

In graduate school, my classmates and I made some colorful ones with paint and feathers and buttons on our papier-mâché faces. That was the messy part: molding our faces to that gooey stuff.

The other students were hard at work describing themselves and appeared to enjoy the stimulating exercise in self-expression. But I was at a complete loss. *How shall I decorate my face?* Unable to make a visual of who I was, I just chose random items to do something, a feather here, a bead there, as though I had a purpose.

I ended up with a red face, a purple mouth, green eyes, and yellow eyebrows, a mask that didn't even vaguely resemble me.

Well, of course not. The woman on the outside was attractive and accomplished: I'd traveled and seen much of the world, I'd raised three children to adulthood, and I'd worked at a satisfying teaching career, culminating now with completing two years of graduate school.

The inside me, the adult child, the addict afraid of her own shadow, had been hidden. I kept what I considered to be my ugliness out of sight. But the mask I made with my school class-mates revealed my dark side.

By 2005, with three years of early work in recovery, I was starting to face up to it. I was taking the first of many moral inventories I would take—Step Four in my recovery program.

What I've discovered over the years is that under the murky darkness lies a simplicity that we can uncover by peeling away our coping mechanisms, our defenses, our strategies for living. We then see ourselves as we once were, in all our softness and light. And stripped down to our purest form is a lovely innocence.

WELL, IT'S
FIVE O'CLOCK
SOMEWHERE

C aroline used to stay with me in the condo when she was back East. She had several friends in the area and enjoyed reconnecting with them. One year for Thanksgiving all of my children were in the area.

Annie had been in and out of recovery for three years, but that year she was out. She came over sometime during the day with her boyfriend, who hid in the basement passed out on the carpet. He never made it upstairs for turkey, and I wonder why she brought him at all.

Caroline was there and so was Carter. The three of them were civil, even chatty, and I opened a bottle of white wine at around eleven in the morning and never stopped drinking it.

No one confronted the corpse in the basement.

I was the mother, the hostess, accepting the situation like it was normal.

But I drank white wine all day until Carter, Annie, and her boyfriend left. Caroline left the house with them and borrowed my car to meet some friends.

After cleaning up the kitchen, I went to bed early, just collapsed on my bed, with a splitting headache.

Caroline woke up the next day and commented, "Well, that was weird yesterday."

NUTS

Shortly after Annie's addiction to methamphetamine became apparent, her father and I put her through a rehabilitation facility in Maryland. It opened her eyes, but thirty days isn't enough for many hard-core drug addicts. Afterward, she moved into a sober living house with a bunch of recovering addicts, discovered cocaine while she was there with those recovering addicts, and soon was on my doorstep again, trying to distance herself from them.

Living with me didn't keep her safe. She brought her demons with her. If something wasn't nailed down, it was gone. That's how I lost much of my mother's silver.

Finally, I kicked her out.

Annie was resourceful. She drifted around, crashing with friends, sleeping on sofas. She had a new boyfriend, a heroin addict named Jim, and he convinced her to move to Richmond with him to get away from prying family eyes. It was ninety minutes away—not that far.

"Hi, Mom," she said, calling me from her new apartment. "Why don't you drive down on Saturday?"

I felt thrilled that she wanted to see me. "Sure, what time? Do you need me to bring you anything?"

"No, just come for lunch. You can take us out."

"Okay, I'll be there at noon."

Annie had met Jim just six months before. She'd been living in Adams Morgan, one of her old haunts. After she left and moved to Richmond with Jim, Angel got a frantic phone call from her landlord saying the television and many appliances had been stolen.

When I met him for lunch the next day, we just looked at each other and sank into further heartache about our daughter. Not in love anymore but still loving each other deeply, we were never more connected than when we were watching our daughter slip away.

Driving to Richmond that Saturday, I didn't have any illusions that she had gotten her life back together. But I wasn't prepared for what she told me.

At the restaurant we made chitchat, ordering lasagna and chatting about Jim's freelance carpentry work. Annie was still looking for a job. I told her Carter was leaving for Austin in June to go to graduate school. No response from her; she was distracted.

Annie and Jim held hands and looked at each other nervously. Something was not right. I felt like they were performing for me, like they were trying to throw me off the scent of their drug use.

"I have news, Mom. I hope you'll be happy for us. We're getting married!"

I experienced immediate shock, trying to process two thoughts:

The wishful thinking: *Oh, I'm so happy. They must be clean now. They must be well enough to think beyond the next five minutes, the next fix.*

And the hard-nosed reality: *Oh my God, she is clearly out of her mind. She has really lost it this time.*

My second thought won, but I didn't have the courage to say anything and spoil lunch.

"So happy for you, honey," I lied, avoiding any eye contact. "Oh gosh, look at the time! I've gotta rush off. Lots of papers to correct. Here's some money for lunch," I offered, leaving fifty dollars on the table. "Will you take care of the bill? Call me tomorrow, and we'll talk more about this."

I gave them both a quick hug as I left the table. Running to my car in a blur, I couldn't get away fast enough.

In the car I was sick with worry. And helpless. What power did I have to change her mind?

Married? I moaned. *This was becoming a worse nightmare.*

Total Wine wasn't far from my condo, and I popped in there for an economy-size bottle of Chardonnay, not even waiting for the change. The twist-off cap let me start right there in the parking lot. I had lacked the courage to be honest at lunch; alcohol was how I was finding my courage more and more those days. The courage to watch my daughter fall into the rabbit hole of drug addiction and be helpless to stop her.

Mirror, mirror . . . I was following her down that hole.

By the time Gene got home, I'd finished about half of the bottle and was terribly drunk, dizzy, and sprawled on the sofa, wailing out loud.

"I'll never do this again, make me promise! This is the last time!"

Gene just held my hand.

DAD

Several months later, Annie was arrested in Baltimore for grand larceny car theft and was placed in the psych ward for observation. When I called there for information, they told me she had checked herself out.

She was lost to us all for a year. No word. She just vanished.

The following winter, Angel hired a detective to find her. He couldn't stand not knowing what had happened to her.

It didn't take the detective long. We learned from him that Annie had coaxed a friend in Baltimore into getting her out of the psych ward. She was living in a suburb of Baltimore with an older man. He took care of her.

And she did whatever was necessary.

Angel drove to the address himself to confront her. He never spoke to me about what had happened when he found her there. But she told her father to come back in a week and she would leave with him. She kept her word.

God, he was brave.

"HOW IS ANNIE, MARILEA?"

My unmasking was not complete. I never talked to my mother about my addictive disease. Unable, as well, to tell her the truth about my daughter's drug addiction, I wore those lies like faded hats until the day she died.

My Oscar-caliber performance went something like this:

"How is Annie, Marilea?" Mother would ask.

"Oh, she's in school in San Francisco studying hotel management. She sends her love though. Wishes she could be here."

It tore at me like a scab that couldn't heal: that ever-present falsehood to quell my mother's need to know about one of her favorite grandchildren. Every time I saw her in the nursing home, she asked me the same question.

Three years into her disease, in the spring of 2005, Annie pulled herself together long enough to take a plane to Boston to see her grandmother. It was the last time she would see her alive.

The two of them had always been particularly close. More than once as a teenager, Annie had abandoned her friends and activities during the summer to fly to Massachusetts to spend time with my mother.

But lying to my mother, was I really fooling her? She came

from a long line of reticent people, people who didn't talk about unpleasant things. My mother must have known I was hiding something. Yet she never pressed me for answers.

What composure. What a lesson in letting go.

I couldn't tell her my secrets. What purpose would it have served? She was ninety-nine years old, wondering every night if she would wake up the next day.

Or maybe I was still a slave to appearances, trying to save face, afraid of confronting her with such bitter disappointments. I was not quite the daughter she was so proud of, and neither was her granddaughter.

She took her thoughts to her grave. In so many fundamental ways, my mother never knew me or my daughter. But I like to believe that, sitting on her perch up in heaven, she is all-knowing of us mortals struggling down here on earth. And she is forgiveness and love, for death cleanses us all.

My mother had lived long enough to understand the futility of dwelling on regrets. She became one of my most powerful teachers.

Maybe when we meet again, we'll hold hands and laugh at all the time we spent chasing butterflies, wanting what we couldn't have, reaching for the stars under the light of a full moon.

DISSOLVED

I'd been enjoying a successful teaching career in Virginia for nearly seventeen years. At school, I tried to throw myself into my students and my work. But after Annie was arrested, I started falling apart.

"Are you all right, miss?" Letsi shouted from the back of the room. When I didn't answer right away, she left her seat and came up to the projector to steady me. My pen had fallen out of my hands, which were visibly shaking.

"Oh, I'm fine, Letsi," I answered, brushing her off. "Please, go back to your seat. Let's finish the lesson, kids." I was starting to feel ill.

"You know, class," I said, smiling, "I'm not feeling well right now and need to run to the bathroom for a minute. While I'm out of the classroom, please copy down the notes on the projector, and we'll go over them when I get back." I left the classroom in a hurry.

Aching with shame and embarrassment, I ran out the door and made it to the bathroom just in time. I had entered a state of dissolving after the policeman called me from Baltimore. That January of 2008, I felt my insides soften. I was barely able to swallow food, and my bowel movements and taste buds had changed—I couldn't stand sweets! Back in the classroom, I made it through to the last class period, but most days were the same. Lying on my bed at home, I stared at the wall for hours at a time. I had lost my passion and interest in many things that used to give me pleasure. Clinical depression was a kind of depression I'd not experienced before.

In the throes of it, I started seeing a psychiatrist. He prescribed an antidepressant to help with the symptoms, and I was able to start eating and pull myself together after a couple of weeks. But the change in me, strange and frightening, was profound.

Against the advice of my doctor, I decided to take early retirement at the end of the school year. My once-beautiful daughter had been sinking into the mire of drug addiction for too long. She was riding high on that hell-bent roller coaster and enduring the inevitable valleys as well. But she wasn't alone. I couldn't bear to watch her commit suicide like that; I was sitting right next to her. When she was arrested in Baltimore, it was time for me to get off the ride and make some changes in my life.

"Marilea, I heard you had put in for retirement. Not so soon! What can I say to talk you out of it?" My colleague Jim was visiting my room at lunchtime.

"Oh, you're sweet, Jim. You know, I never talk about it cuz so many of us boomers are going through the same thing with our aging parents. My mother is ninety-eight years old in a nursing home, and it's not fair to my sister and brother to handle things on their own. I need to be there more often to help out. The guilt has been killing me."

"Oh sure, I'm with you there. My parents are in Montana, and I feel guilty all the time. Well, we sure will miss you here, Marilea. Wish I could change your mind," he said, offering me a hug.

"Thanks, Jim," I said, warmly returning his hug. *Oh, how I'll miss it here—my dear colleagues and students. I'm walking away from my dream job. How I wish I could tell someone the real reason why.*

But I was afraid. And lying. Hiding.

The stigma our country places on addiction and mental health is powerful. I remembered the breakdown I had thirty-five years earlier, when I was living in Cambridge and going to art school. Mr. Jones's words had been, "Marilea, go home. You're just exhausted and need to stop working and rest."

The principal of the school where I worked was a kind and caring man. He might have said the same thing. It was as if the Cambridge breakdown had been a dress rehearsal for the real show.

A month before I looked at my classroom for the last time, the administrative staff thanked another colleague and me for our years of service. In all my seventy years, it remains one of my most poignant memories.

THE INSIDER

Mother gave me her set of Haviland Limoges china when I became a diplomat's wife in 1976. How she loved the ring of those words, "diplomat's wife." She was so proud of me, and she wanted me to use the best items when I was entertaining and representing our country overseas. But I only had service for twelve, not enough for all the guests at our dinners. I had to borrow the embassy china. So my handsome set of Limoges sat in my pantry, lonely and collecting dust, except for an occasional holiday meal over the next thirty-two years— until I retired from teaching. That's when I actually needed a teacup.

I could have brought a mug or a plain teacup. Colorful mugs with cheeky sayings fill my cupboards from all my travels. But I thought I'd dust off one of my mother's teacups for a tea the school was having in my honor. *In my honor* . . . imagine that! This was a real tea with scones, cucumber sandwiches, and people who came to wish me well in my new life.

Mother was thrilled when I told her. She felt that in some way my life had come full circle, as if it had revolved around her Limoges china. And in some ways my adult life had.

I'd been a teacher for nearly twenty years. But in my first years as a teacher overseas, I had little or no idea what I was doing. It wasn't until I was teaching in a first-rate school district with excellent professional development opportunities that I learned how to teach well in a classroom. So much of the person I'd evolved into at that time centered on my work. Teaching day and night for a while, I loved my high school. But when my children all left home within six months of each other in 2000, I had no distractions from my work. For the next eight years, it consumed me. It wasn't going to be easy to jump off the fast track.

But I made my decision and prepared to retire from full-time teaching. A few people didn't want me to leave, but I still hoped to fade away without a fuss. No such luck! This shy woman who avoided attention, who once lost her voice on the stage when it was time for her solo, became a star for a few hours.

"Please join us to wish a cherished colleague a happy retirement," the invitation read. *Cherished!* I was surprised by the word. This looked like my moment in the sun, and I wanted to enjoy it. What better symbol of my self-regard in the profession, my worth as an educator that had come at great personal cost, than to share my mother's Limoges, not a Styrofoam cup, at a celebration in my honor.

The making of this china is arduous, like many hard-won accomplishments. But I'm glad I brought my mother's china teacup. Her words had taken on a new meaning for me: "Don't be afraid to do what's difficult," she had advised me in Greece when she learned I was divorcing Angel. "Even if it seems hard, you'll be a stronger person for it."

Teaching and learning: that endless hermeneutic circle that defines much of who I would become as an adult.

EXCUSES, EXCUSES

L osing Annie wasn't improving my character; it was crushing me.

I'd been drinking more and more, developing a taste for vodka and wine. Gene, his face duct-taped from ear to ear, watched and waited, always ready to catch me if I fell. He knew better than anyone that words could be counterproductive with addicts. Often, they just spurred us on.

Once, while trying to get the wine out of a bottle, I nearly cut off my thumb.

Many times, my lowered inhibitions from a glass or two of wine sent me wandering to the refrigerator when I wasn't hungry.

Weddings: champagne, slurred speech, embarrassment.

Ocean City: vodka and junk food on the boardwalk.

Annie's battle with heroin: white wine, economy-size.

Too much alcohol: missed steps, sprained ankles.

Over the course of twenty-six years, there hadn't been that many episodes. But alcoholism is a cunning predator.

And it's a progressive disease.

How many incidents would I need to string together before I ended up like my father, dead before my time?

INTERIORS

Mother always told me to pick up things that were lying on the floor—it didn't matter what, just get it off the floor—as though not seeing something would make it go away.

But that just transferred the mess somewhere else.

A FAMILY DISEASE

So much to say. And so much not to say!
Some things are better left unsaid. But so many
unsaid things can become a burden.

—Virginia M. Axline[17]

Mother died in her sleep eighteen months after my retirement. Five months after the memorial service, I visited my sister.

"Marilea, I'm in the basement. After you finish your coffee, come down here and let's go through as much as we can this morning."

"Sure, I'll be right there," I said, not looking forward to the division of our mother's personal property.

We looked at every scarf, every skirt, and every jacket. I didn't like Mother's taste in clothes, nor did anything fit me, and though Lucy salvaged some things for herself, most of the clothes went to Goodwill. I took some books and other small items. There was a lamp and a table in Lucy's attic that I wanted, and they fit in my car, so she gave them to me. The family albums were hard to divide up; we spent a couple of hours that morning xeroxing pages that we both wanted so we could each have them.

As we were finishing up our work for the morning, my sister approached me and looked me right in the eyes.

"Marilea, there's something I've been meaning to tell you. When Mother became pregnant with you, quite unexpectedly, she was so overwhelmed at the thought of having another baby that she sent me to live in New York with Aunt Lila for about a year. Apparently, she couldn't manage Bill, me, and a new baby. So I lived there before we all moved up to Massachusetts."

I felt as though I had been hit with a jackhammer. Suddenly, the puzzle pieces were jarred loose inside of me, and they tumbled out all at once.

My mother had never been able to tell me her secret. By the time I came along in 1948, she was thirty-eight, approaching middle age and still living in New Jersey. Depressed a lot of the time, with a husband who disappointed her, she found it daunting to be having a third child. Somehow her life didn't seem so overwhelming with one less child in the house for a little while.

My sister did me a valuable service by telling me our mother's secret. So much of what I'd lived through as a child at last made sense; now there was no more mystery. I understood why I'd felt like an intruder, why my addition to our family seemed too much for my parents to handle effectively.

And I feel such compassion for them both, caught up in the maelstrom of alcoholism.

GENERATIONS

M other and Dad were good, well-intentioned people. Learning about their experiences growing up has rewarded me with a great deal of understanding toward them.

My mother grew up in the shadow of her beautiful sister. Both girls triangulated with their mother. Sometimes sides were taken, and my mother felt left out. Later on as a parent, she became a demanding perfectionist, beating back the pain of self-doubt and unworthiness by raising accomplished children.

My father's childhood was much worse. His father stayed at the Harvard Club, not always living at home with my grandmother and their four children. I don't remember ever meeting him.

Dad was hit with a baseball bat as a child and had to wear a pair of thick glasses. Other children taunted him often, calling him "four-eyes." Because of his eyesight, he was never able to enlist in World War II with all the other patriotic men in America. That hurt him a great deal.

My father made attempts later on to give up gin and tobacco. When he had his gall bladder removed, the nurses asked him to cough into a bag. This motivated him to stop smoking for a while. But he was never completely free of those crutches. They were like those cruel children who reminded him of how he felt as a

child with a distant father. "You're not good enough, not important enough." As a young man working in the family business, he
met and fell in love with my mother, who spent a good part of
their marriage echoing his father's disappointment in him.

Families are swallowed whole into the belly of the beast, then
spit out, pieces at a time. When Mom married Dad, his family
became her family as well. She had her own wounds, but without
the benefit of a recovery program, the pain persisted. Many of us
in my alcoholic family were wounded souls.

AUNT MEG

When I saw Aunt Meg for the last time, she was living in an elegant facility in Massachusetts. We had lunch there, and then I walked her to her room before leaving. Sitting down in her favorite chair, she winced when I held her hands to steady her.

"I don't mind being this old, Marilea, really, I don't. But one of the hardest parts for me is living with the pain."

"Oh, I'm sorry, Meg."

I didn't know what else to say. I knew she had terrible arthritis, as did my father. It runs in my family, and now I'm troubled by it.

It's funny the things we remember. Those words, "living with the pain," remind me that I'm just another in a long line of alcoholics. My father and his eldest sister were close when they were young. And, not surprisingly, they both turned to alcohol to deal with life's pressures and disappointments.

Aunt Meg was my godmother. In my Episcopal family, godparents gifted their godchildren with a prayer book. The one she gave me, inscribed with love, is with me wherever I'm living. As my godmother, she felt spiritually responsible for me.

She had been in recovery for many years before she died, one of the most admirable success stories in our family. Drinking alcoholically all those years, and unable to be honest with Meg about our connection, I had missed an opportunity to learn and grow from a valued family member. It was another example of how, within my own family, I hid the truth from those around me. How I wish I'd been able to trust more and be honest with those who loved me!

She was another of my angels. I carry her example with me always.

HURRICANES

Gene had retired from teaching within a year of my retirement, and we opted for a change of scenery. I did the groundwork, and one weekend we flew to New Mexico to buy a little house between Albuquerque and Santa Fe. We pooled our resources, pitching in together all we had. Gene and some friends cleared the back quarter acre of sagebrush, and he bought a dozen fruit trees to start an orchard. Over the years, he's planted and nurtured a total of fifty trees—Rainier cherries, Saturn peaches, Challengers, Shiro plums, apricots, and many kinds of apples. One year we had so many peaches we had to give them away. It was grueling work but gratifying as we watched the blossoms turn into fruit.

Throwing myself into full-time recovery in New Mexico, I began the process of new growth in myself, attending one or two recovery meetings a day. That became my full-time job, embracing a spiritual way of life. But it's come with a steep learning curve.

In Virginia, when I first started going to meetings, the guidelines of the program were hard for me to follow. I felt responsible for what was happening to Annie and couldn't let go of my need to save her, unwilling to admit my powerlessness. Doing so seemed counterintuitive to me.

Late in 2002, after we had sent her to her first rehab, she did well for a little while. I remember saying this at a recovery meeting:

"I have no doubt that my daughter's progress parallels my own." The people at the meeting just nodded, recognizing that was where I needed to be in that moment.

Still attached to my daughter with no understanding of the concepts of detachment and letting go, I thought I held all the cards—the magic bullet to her recovery. I desperately needed to believe that.

In time, though, I accepted that addiction is a brain disease— still a matter of much controversy in this country—and not a moral failing. Annie was sick. I had no more power over her illness than if she'd had diabetes or cancer.

Through trial and error, following the road map that had helped many addicts and families of addicts since the 1950s, I learned to let go of the things no longer in my control. I wanted to find the lost child that I had left in the woods in the town by the lake.

And I needed to get on with my life. But I had one more thing to surrender, one more thing to place at the altar of my God.

TORN

B ack in the 1980s, a neighbor gave Mother a bunch of Polly Flinders dresses, and I dressed both girls in that beautiful embroidered clothing for several years—until they protested loudly and refused to put on another dress. They grew up and, in their twenties, went their separate ways.

But in the autumn of 2010, both of them became seriously ill.

Caroline was in the hospital in San Francisco with a bad case of Crohn's disease. Annie was back East in the hospital where doctors were madly trying to save her femoral artery.

They were three thousand miles apart, and I was in the middle, in New Mexico.

"Please don't worry," Caroline assured me over the phone, "I'm being well taken care of. Really, I'll be fine."

"I'll be on the next flight."

After arriving at San Francisco Airport and getting to the Mission District where she lived, I let myself in to her apartment with the key she'd hidden for me and left my things there. On my way to San Francisco General, I stopped in a park to rest a bit before facing her. It was within walking distance of her apartment.

I sat there on a gorgeous October day, remembering how chilly it got in San Francisco in the summer with the marine layer hovering over it. Autumn is the best time to go to that splendid city, I decided. Trying hard to hold it together, I focused on the beauty all around me.

Both of my girls were in hospitals, both in serious condition. For ten years I'd been struggling with them in different ways, and, in that moment, I was shedding many tears. I was remembering how Lucy and I had grown up in the same family but so alienated and distant from each other. I had sworn that my two girls would grow up differently. I'd vowed to myself that they would be close. And they had been for years.

But now they were many miles apart from each other. Caroline had finished college and was enjoying her life on the West Coast. Annie had also finished college but was living as a drug addict on the East Coast.

I recognized the truth of it and maybe for the first time had accepted that they were worlds apart from each other.

Hurrying to the hospital to see my daughter, I dried my eyes, put on a smile, and went up to Caroline's room.

"Hi, baby! Oh, look at you. You're skin and bones!" I said, trying not to sound as alarmed as I felt.

"Yeah, well, they have to starve me to get a good look at my intestines. But it's not so bad."

Oh, my baby is so brave. If only I could trade places with her.

"How bad?" I asked. I didn't believe her.

"On a scale of one to ten, my Crohn's is an eight. I guess it is pretty bad. I didn't want you to worry. But there are lots of treatments they'll start experimenting with. I'll be fine. You can go check on Annie."

"I'm staying a week until it's clear you'll be okay, Caroline. No argument."

"Okay, Mama. I'm really glad you're here." She seemed tired but grateful.

I'd made my choice.

THAT DAMN
DRAWER

Just 'cause you got the monkey off your back
doesn't mean the circus has left town.

—George Carlin[18]

I thought I had patched myself up pretty well and gotten all of my addictions under control. Here in my third act, I believed I'd finally gotten it together. I didn't dare have any more human frailties. I had to be strong for my children. But it wasn't that simple. It's like the bureau when you push one drawer in and another drawer springs out.

Someone was laughing up in heaven, maybe my dad.

"More will be revealed," it says somewhere in the recovery literature.

That's for sure.

CLEANING HOUSE

*Step Ten: Continued to take personal inventory
and when we were wrong promptly admitted it.*[19]

O ne of the most important tools of my recovery has been accepting responsibility for my actions and not blaming others for my problems. The next step from there is to make amends to anyone I may have injured in my life. Guilt is a particularly disruptive emotion; when left alone, it has eaten away at my self-esteem and left me vulnerable over the years.

I had to make many amends. One of the first people I apologized to was my sister.

On a visit to Massachusetts, I told Lucy something that was decades overdue.

I took her hands in mine and looked her in the eyes.

"I'm so sorry, Lucy, for all my bratty behavior when I was little. I didn't respect your space, I broke your figurines, I took your shoes. I'm so sorry."

"And you were never punished for it."

Those words spilling out of her mouth surprised me, but I didn't let go of her hands. I searched her eyes, looking for clarification, and I found it.

"At the time," she said, slowly mulling over her words, "you were not punished for it."

Caroline and Carter were next on my list. Throughout Annie's addiction, I'd been obsessed with saving her, putting my other children in the background. I needed to make some serious amends about that, as well as my neglect during their childhood and so much of their upbringing. Their response to me has been kind.

"Mom," Carter said, "of course I forgive you. I love you very much. But it's better for me if I don't dwell on my childhood. You need to stop bringing it up."

I'm powerless to erase the parts of his childhood that cause him pain; but it's necessary for me to accept that he has his own ways of coping with what happened to him, and to let it go.

"Mom, it's okay. I forgive you," Caroline offered generously. "I get that you had stuff to deal with. Let's move on from it. Just know that I love you now and appreciate the efforts you're making."

I was not as fortunate with Annie five years ago.

I sent her an e-mail because I didn't have an address to mail her a letter. This was Annie's response:

Your "amends"??? Sure, I could use a laugh. And by the way, if you think a couple warm, fuzzy e-mails ERASE the last 2–3 YEARS of you treating me like SHIT (ESPE-CIALLY when I've been doing everything you and Dad wanted me to do, i.e., become financially independent), then you are WRONG. I've believed ever since I was in elementary school that you are a JOKE of a parent not to mention UTTERLY full of shit, and the fact that you've had the NERVE to e-mail me the last 3–4 years WITH-OUT apologizing for the atrocious shit you've done and said to me in the last couple years certainly confirms my long-held beliefs about you. Of COURSE I ended up on drugs. I had YOU for a mother.

When I shared this with my sponsor, she reminded me of something vital to my recovery: when we make amends to someone, we do it for the cleansing of our own souls, not for any anticipated outcome.

It's freeing to remember that, especially when I can still feel stung and shaken by Annie's harsh words. I can't do anything about the past, nor can I make her see that my attempts to help her, though often misguided, sprang from my love for her.

And the best amends, I believe, are not even found in words. They are living amends.

We can't change the past, but we can try to do things differently now.

Step Ten invites me to grow up, to be responsible, and to make amends—all for my own benefit. I take Step Ten because I want to be the best me I can be.[20]

BEFORE

Several years before I attempted to make amends to Annie, she was in her last rehab in California. It was 2009, and I flew across the country for Parents' Weekend. After excitedly showing me around the grounds, she bumped into a couple of new friends.

"Hey, Annalise, show us more of those moves."

My daughter still enjoyed showing people what she had been able to do as a gymnast in Greece.

"Sure." Proud of her agility, she showed us, among other things, a backward twist that must have been difficult then. She wasn't ten anymore.

As she leaned backward toward the floor, her hair fell back; I saw the scar again and wondered how she'd gotten it. She must have had an accident to have sustained such a deep gash around her hairline in the middle of her forehead.

When Annie was a child, she looked like a beautiful mandarin doll. She'd always had a thick pile of bangs to frame her oval face. But her hair didn't fall that way anymore because of the scar, and she hadn't been wearing bangs for several years. I remembered the picture of my children from JCPenney's one Christmas in Miami, her pretty brown eyes accented by her thick bangs.

Seeing her then in rehab, I focused on her bangs. How much

I missed seeing them on her! What mother doesn't mourn her child's innocence and wish a painless life for her?

The last time I saw her, in 2012, I was in a San Francisco motel near the hostel in the Tenderloin where she was staying. She was to spend a night with me and had a key to the room. It was five in the morning when I heard her unlocking the door, and I jumped up to open it.

"Hi, Mom. This is Pontus."

"Hi there," the much older man said as he offered to shake my hand.

"Hello, Pontus. Annie, please come in now so I can go back to sleep."

"Sure, Mom. See you later, Buddy."

I have a picture of her sitting on my bed the next morning, her terrier, Loki, on her lap; she was never without him. Her hair was pulled to the side and held with a clip, exposing the scar.

She looked so strange—like someone else—without those lustrous bangs. But of course she was . . . someone else.

OWNING IT

For a long time I thought if I wasn't rotting in jail from a DUI, or falling down a flight of stairs, or passed out on the sofa while the grandkids were drinking Clorox, I didn't have an alcohol problem. Certainly, there had to be a catastrophe to prove that I was an alcoholic. Hell, I could go years without a drink and not miss it. So I couldn't be an alcoholic, I assumed, because I could live without it.

Until I chose not to. Until the day when a friend might come for a weeklong visit, I'd get a fifth of vodka and drink it in my walk-in closet like it was water. Why?

My insecurities, my unmet expectations, my fragile ego . . .

That's when I should have been paying attention. Alcohol had become another dirty little secret.

I'd been toying with alcohol with increased frequency since the divorce, though I'd binged on it a few times beforehand, usually over the holidays when I couldn't shoulder my guilt or when the drunken holidays from my childhood revisited me.

But it was still so occasional that I didn't take it seriously. My alcohol use was slipping under the radar of acceptability. I never missed a day of work; there weren't many incidents. But the few I did indulge in were doozies.

Several years ago while visiting friends in San Francisco, I got remarkably smashed on tequila at a Mexican restaurant. Our friends and I had already had two glasses of wine before Gene and I left for the restaurant in the city. They had an errand to run beforehand, so we went in separate cars.

On the way back to the house, I started screaming at Gene.

"You son of a bitch! I hate you. How dare you patronize me like that in front of our friends!"

"Marilea, I wasn't patronizing you. I told you to slow down on the margaritas, and when you wouldn't, I thought it best to go home."

"Stop the car. I want to get out. I can't stand to look at you!"

My guardian angel still hung around, fortunately, and soon after that we pulled into our friend's driveway.

Gene put me to bed and hoped I would sleep it off. I did.

That man should be nominated for sainthood.

It never happened again, so he let it go. Maybe he was giving me a pass because of what had been happening with Annie. Perhaps a number of people were. But we alcoholics will tell you that we'll always have a ready-made excuse.

Because we never really need one.

REBEL

It seemed to happen overnight, my baby, Caroline, changing from a compliant preppy twelve-year-old, wearing nothing but Benetton, into an angry alienist.

Blame the heavy metal music from the 1980s: Tipper Gore said it was destroying our youth.

Goths. All the black. Those eyes like racoons. That pungent patchouli oil.

She had green hair when she was a freshman and didn't enjoy high school. She refused to walk with her class in 1999. A year later she and her best friend took off in her Mazda for San Francisco, as far as she could get away from me without falling into the Pacific Ocean. I let her go without a fuss because in my mind that's what good parents do: they let their children go. But I remember thinking, *She's still mad at me about cutting her lice-infested hair in Greece when she was six.*

For a while she lived in a pink house in Haight-Ashbury, long after Haight-Ashbury housed the Grateful Dead and a lot of other rebels.

Twenty years and many letters later, she has a good life there. But I'm insatiable. Though I'd already made amends to her, I asked her again last year, "Have you really forgiven me for being such a neglectful mom?" I was hoping for another nice answer.

"Of course I forgive you, Mama. I rely on you more than anyone else."

I love my sweet Cal, my flower child.

KARMA

Our first house in Virginia boasted an outdoor speaker system so we could listen to music on the patio. But it was broken, and we never had it fixed.

Instead, the speaker provided a nesting place for a number of birds in the six years we lived there. Every spring, forgetting that it was right next to our kitchen door but high enough for the birds to feel safe from curious humans, I would start to notice the flight of a couple of birds back and forth to the same spot. And there was a maple tree in front of our fence where one of the birds often sat, waiting its turn to be a parent.

"They're back!" I yelped to my neighbor, who was pulling up weeds. I felt foolish, tipping the birds off.

"I want to see how many eggs she's laid, Angel. Please bring the ladder outside," I asked as he was hanging up a picture in the dining room.

"Don't be crazy. If they see you go anywhere near their nest, they'll abandon it."

So I left it alone, watching Mom and Pop swoop in and take turns sitting on the eggs.

One May morning I heard a lot of chirping coming from inside the broken speaker, and I observed the parents, one at a time, bringing food to their hatchlings. Such a simple cooperative effort, ensuring the welfare of their young.

Hatchlings became nestlings, and then came the end of the swooping. There were no more parents taking turns at the nest, and the comforting sounds of life, the chirping, had stopped.

I realized the babies must have been strong enough to leave the nest and test their wings. They had become fledglings, and they were off.

But I saw the female soon afterward in the maple nearby singing.

Gosh, those baby birds must be miles away by now. And there was Mom hovering nearby, probably thinking the same thing.

Still I wonder, sometimes, if they can hear their mother singing.

BIRTHDAYS

"Cate," I declared at a dinner for my granddaughter's eighth birthday, "I know I live close now so my being here for your birthday is not such a big deal. But if I lived in Alaska, I'd still come for your birthday."

"I know," she said, looking at me solemnly. "The only time you missed was during that blizzard in Virginia when I was two."

"That's right. I never miss birthdays."

I was so touched that she remembered the one time I'd missed.

Like it mattered.

Then she climbed onto my lap and hugged me.

"I love you, Bela."

Then I knew that I mattered.

DUXBURY

Lining up all my conches and other shells like students in a classroom, I'm mindful of what they are teaching me.

Once I waded into a cave in the sea around Greece and found a large cache of sea urchin tests, or exoskeletons, long since abandoned by their hosts. When my family left Athens in 1990, I packed them as carefully as my mother's Limoges china, but I've loved them more.

The most beautiful shell I have used to sit on the window seat in my mother's hillside home in Massachusetts. We found it at dead low tide one hot summer day at Duxbury Beach when I was seven. She had held on to that conch for over fifty years, maybe for the same reason I have trouble throwing my shells away: the assurance that something of us is left behind.

From each of my beach excursions, I've made sure to bring back a shell or two. And in the fifty years that I've been amassing my collection, I've run out of space to display them.

Now, my son chides me, I must leave shells where they are—and driftwood too—to shore up the beach.

LEMONADE

When I go back to Massachusetts for a visit, Lucy and I usually swap clothes and jewelry. My sister is generous with me.

Once I bought a stunning turquoise bracelet for thirty-five dollars at her favorite thrift store. She was with me, and I noticed how much she admired it.

I took it home and never wore it. Ever.

But I held on to it just for spite.

A few years ago, I was ready to let go of my spite and the bracelet. I offered it to her on a visit, and she was happy to accept it.

But the swapping of shoes, that has more meaning for us. She can't wear my shoes because we're not the same size anymore. But sometimes I can wear hers. She gave me a pair of $150 Dansko clogs she might have worn once that I would wear all the time when I worked as a substitute teacher in New Mexico.

And I still wear a pair of black suede ankle boots she gave me a decade ago. They're falling apart from so much use, but I can't bear to part with them.

She used to collect shoes like I collected seashells. We both had many more than we needed.

But the issue of shoes cut a wide swath in our lives.

Healing comes in many forms.

ANOTHER ANGEL

A ngel died suddenly from complications of esophageal cancer almost four years ago, and with his passing I've lost one of my touchstones. My former husband had become one of my dearest friends. We had so much shared history that he couldn't help but be a large part of my narrative. He was right beside me in many of my travels, an unwitting witness to my search for fulfillment. And though our marriage had become stormy toward the end, I learned with him how to navigate a relationship that was once full of passion and promise. We had all the best reasons in the world to stay together: our three beautiful children. It was seeing the hurt in them that brought us closest together and tested us in ways that might have torn many parents apart.

As we watched our middle child, Annie, lose herself in the seductive underworld of drug addiction, all the turmoil from our marriage faded away and was forgotten. We were never closer or more appreciative of each other.

I've seen couples—married or otherwise—sear the flesh off one another watching an addicted child flounder. There's plenty of blame to go around, and it's only natural to question our parenting and shoulder responsibility. But Angel and I never walked down that dead-end street. Year after year of Annie's roller coaster ride to hell, we bonded more. When she ran away to Richmond with Jim, we met to talk about it over lunch. Our hearts ached in unison as we watched her succumb to the living death of heroin addiction. Angel became the dear friend I'd been hoping to cherish for many more years.

"Marilea, meet me in the lobby at noon tomorrow. I have some papers to go over with you. And I just want to see how you're doing. Can you make it?"

"I'll be there. Look forward to it." I smiled to myself, almost tumbling back in time to the carefree years of courtship before life happened to us.

We occasionally met during his lunch hour to share wine and pasta at his favorite restaurant near the Rand Corporation, where he was working. Both in happy and stable relationships, we were able to steal ourselves away from our grief over Annie long enough to remember some good times. Laughing together in the nearly empty restaurant, we enjoyed reminiscing about the kids in the early 1980s when they were little.

"Angel," I'd asked my husband most evenings, "I'm tired. Please put the kids to bed."

He'd either watch television with them or read them their favorite books. Then, one by one, he carried them up to bed and kissed them goodnight. And though he was dedicated to going to Carter's many sports events, I reminded him, laughing, of how he spent most of his attendance with his head in a book.

Angel was not a perfect husband or a perfect father, but he did his best. If ever there was a measure for our esteem toward one another, it was in our love for our children.

These lunches were special occasions for two people who had once thought they would never be apart. Through all the broken dreams, we found a way to heal our relationship. And our divorce became a glorious example of friendship at its best.

An unexpected miracle.

THE TALK

Three years ago, my son and his wife asked me to come down to their home. They had something important to talk about with me. As I was walking in, I remembered that it was a weekday.

"Why aren't you two at work today?"

"This was more important, Mom. Come sit down. We need to talk."

Uh-oh. I felt myself cringing. *I know that tone of voice so well. The one from my French professor who noticed parts of my term paper sounded a lot like the blurb on the jacket of a novel.*

My fear was growing.

"Mom, we know you've been drinking vodka from our supply behind the bar downstairs. The bottles are nearly empty, and no one else here drinks vodka."

Naked . . . naked . . . naked. I felt like I'd been skinned alive, with everything beneath the surface exposed, scenes from *Predator* making me nauseous. There was nothing I could do. I felt so ugly.

"Mom, what is going on with you? Is it Annie? Why do you need to drink secretly like that? Why don't you drink upstairs with us? No big deal."

Next, the avalanche of tears: the divorce, the angry and depressed children. Carter and Carrie rushed to my side, supporting me, compassionate.

I hung my head in shame. What a dreadful and mortifying experience. Humbling.

And, ultimately, edifying.

It was the giant mirror we all fear but at the same time require if we want to be our best in the world.

That did it for me. When I saw the look in their eyes, the worry, distrust, and fear, it was suddenly too high a price to pay for the numbness I got from secretly quaffing large amounts of vodka.

That was the bottom many addicts need to reach before they're willing to stop. And once again, my guardian angel was with me. My bottom might have killed me.

Children, I'm so sorry.

They didn't tell me to stop drinking. That was my decision. I wrote them a letter of amends a week later and hoped they would trust me again in time, these two loving and hopeful mirrors that tell me I can transcend my limitations, that I can embody God's gifts.

I've learned a hard lesson over the years, that the only life I can save is my own. Surrendering my addictions and working on my emotional sobriety continues to ensure a better life for myself. My dear son and daughter-in-law nevertheless played an important role to that end. There's a poignant bond between us now. Though we rarely speak of it—the tamed elephant in the living room—it's there, an invisible thread, quite apart from our family connection. There's an intimacy between us that was never there before.

When my shortcomings had weighed me down for so many years, my son, through the power of his own forgiveness, has given me the chance to change. There's a lightness in my steps now as I enjoy my grandchildren, and when I tell this story at meetings, sometimes with tears flowing around me, it is clear to me how fathers can live in sons.

REFLECTIONS

I look in the mirror through the eyes
of the child that was me.

—Judy Collins, "Secret Gardens"[21]

"Hi, Family, it's good to be back." I was addressing my friends at a recovery meeting on Camano Island after being away for a few weeks.

Joan, sitting to my right, interrupted me, "Who are you?"

"Oh, yes," I said, embarrassed. "My name's Marilea, and I'm an addict/alcoholic."

They all smiled; they knew the drill.

There's a reason why we need to discipline ourselves in this way. It's not a slap on the wrist. It's a reminder.

And we need reminding.

There's an old joke in the Program:

"How do you know an alcoholic is lying?"

"His lips are moving."

We are, hands down, the world's biggest liars, if only to ourselves.

For the past twenty-five years, I'd been drinking alcoholically: I was looking for a buzz to escape from uncomfortable feelings.

But I wasn't being honest with myself.

Denial is common with those of us who love our addictions, and until something is brought out into the light, it's not real. That's how I started dealing with my food addiction: by telling people. Shame took a back seat in favor of honesty. I needed those mirrors around me. They didn't represent judgment or scrutiny; they became support and encouragement. That's why twelve-step fellowships are so successful.

As long as I stop isolating, I will welcome feedback from friends like Joan—unable, finally, to get away with anything.

And that's a good thing.

"Thank you for my recovery," my friend Sally always says to the group at the end of her shares.

STEELY WOMEN

All we are asked to bear we can bear.
That is a law of the spiritual life. The only hindrance
to the working of this law, as of all benign laws, is fear.

—Elizabeth Goudge[22]

M y home recovery group on Camano Island is called Steel
Magnolias. We're a varied group of alcoholic and/or
drug-addicted women. I'm always delighted to see that some of
them are young. They have their whole lives ahead of them and
will have better skills to cope with whatever comes their way.

Sometimes I imagine my forty-year-old daughter sitting
among these women. I lose myself in that dangerous valley of "If
only's."

Then I blink my eyes, and she's gone.

Most of the women there, like me, are on the farther end of
the age spectrum. Why is that? Maybe when we're young, we
haven't experienced enough failures yet, strung together on string
like my shell necklaces, to feel humbled.

To remain teachable, we have to admit—even embrace with
wonder—how much there is in life we still don't know.

POTLUCKS

I'm getting over my shyness, sharing myself with my recovery fellowship in Washington State. When these people ask me to talk at gatherings, I happily accept, glad to be asked. Within this fellowship, it is widely understood that the best way to keep our recovery is by giving it away.

But I still get anxious allowing myself to be so vulnerable before large groups of people.

Even though it wasn't the first time I'd spoken at a gathering, I was nervous, so I called my sponsor.

"Allison, what will I talk about? Why would they want to hear about me?"

"Just tell them where you've been, where you are, and how you got here." I could see her rolling her eyes from 1,500 miles away; she'd told me that before.

I got up to the podium and told them my conversation with Allison, adding that, "I'm seventy years old, so I'd better not be too long-winded about it."

I waited for them to finish laughing to tell my story.

That particular recovery group is called "Rule 62: Don't Take Yourself Too Damn Seriously."

I like that.

GRATITUDE

When we were still living in Virginia and teaching high school, Gene and I used our vacations to visit as many national parks as we could. It was a rare summer when we didn't make a cross-country trip to see the many wonders in our country. Gene knew that I'd seen much of the world but little of my own country, so he was determined to show me.

By 2003, not yet having been to Santa Fe, I wanted to go there. It boasted, among other things, a world-renowned outdoor opera. We got tickets to a performance of *Così Fan Tutte* and flew to Albuquerque in July, starting the hour-long drive to the capital in a rented convertible and a hailstorm.

We had heard about monsoons and could see the darkening sky, but we ignored the warning signs, intent on feeling the wind on our faces. As we drove north with the top down, mothball-sized hailstones pounded onto the pavement, smashing into tiny pellets. Instead of feeling the wind on our faces, we were being stung by a deluge of those projectiles, frantically looking for a newspaper to cover our heads.

"Pull over for Chrissake, Gene! We're getting pelted, and everything's gonna get soaked!"

"There's no place to pull over, Marilea. Hang on. I'll take the next exit."

Somewhere north of the airport, we raced onto an exit ramp and stopped on the side of the road. Scurrying to get the top up, we didn't notice that the hail had suddenly stopped falling and the sun was teasing us, peeking through the clouds.

"Wanna put the top back down, babe?" Gene enjoyed toying with me.

"No," I retorted, picking up the not-yet-melted stones and throwing them out the window. The ride north to Santa Fe was bleak and brown but not dusty thanks to the rain. Nervously looking up at the sky, I was anxious to get there.

At the time, we had no idea that we'd be living in New Mexico five years later. After our retirement in 2008, we decided to make a fresh start out West. That's when we bought a small house and Gene got the trees to start an orchard. We do love living there part of the year, with a view of the mountain turning into a red watermelon at sunset that's panoramic, the reds muting into grays and browns as the sun drops below the western horizon. But, though our house is small, the orchard beckons: pruning, raking, protecting the tree bark from the rabbits' sharp teeth that cause girdling, which kills the trees. All four seasons require different kinds of work, but it's never easy.

So we like to slip away. And fortunately, the "land of enchantment" is, well, enchanting.

One year on a day in late June, we wanted to take a day hike, so it couldn't be too far. We did a little research and got on a highway going west. Turning right on a road north into the mountains, we decided to stop at a trailhead that promised to lead to a beautiful lake.

That particular trail was poorly marked, sending us down to a river when we wanted to go up. It didn't take us long to figure out that we were on our own, and luckily Gene is an expert at reading trails. So we loped along on that warm day in late June, shedding layers of clothing as we climbed—but holding on to them because we'd need them as soon as we stopped moving. Growing grouchy from hunger, I started needling Gene.

"Are you sure there's a lake up there, Gene? Jeez, if I'd known I was gonna be a mountain goat I'd have worn better shoes."

"One day at a time" is one thing, darlin', but your inability to plan anything more than a trip to the grocery store seriously drives me nuts. There I went again, handing him the reins and then blaming him for a wrong turn. I was just tired and hungry. Thank goodness I knew I was being a nag, so I kept my mouth shut.

"I'm pretty sure I saw one on the map, probably over that ridge," he answered, valiantly trying to keep my hope alive.

"Okay, I've already counted fifteen switchbacks. That pristine lake'd better be worth it," I warned, stuffing my mouth with wasabi peas.

I didn't meet Gene until I was middle-aged, and what a ride it's been. My life before him involved little regular exercise. When I was growing up in Massachusetts, I went ice-skating on the lake in the winter and then sledding down a steep hill behind the Unitarian church. But then puberty set in, and I became the couch potato queen of all time. Before I developed eating disorders and became seriously obese, I was just a weight-obsessed teenager trying to stomach skim milk and Lawry's Seasoned Salt. My ambitious mother worried constantly about my appearance and tried hard to get me to exercise.

First, there was skiing. But by the time I was sixteen my thighs had no muscle strength and the most I ever learned to do was snowplow slowly down a short hill. Not much of a workout there. Note to parents: start exercise regimens when children are young; by the time they're teenagers, it can be quite a struggle.

My idea of a walk was down to the end of the street to catch the bus to school. I never walked much anywhere, and as a teenager I drove a car. So that was that, until I totaled it one night and lost that privilege. It didn't motivate me to walk more, though. Just eat more.

Also, there was horseback riding. A few weeks after I started lessons, the horse got spooked by a bird coming out of the woods and threw me on my butt. That pretty much ended my equestrian career. I bruised my tailbone and was laid up much of the time, becoming, almost literally, a couch potato.

But my life with Gene changed me radically in that regard. Exercise of some sort would become a regular part of my life from then on.

We reached the crest of a hill and found ourselves approaching a high meadow. It was a dazzling sight, with vibrant wildflowers everywhere. The air was cool enough to be refreshing, even with the New Mexican sun blazing down on us at midday. The fragrance of the piñons and junipers filled the air, and I felt glad we'd made the effort to get that far.

"So where do you think the lake is, babe?" I asked, in a much better mood without my stomach growling.

"I dunno. But we seem to be approaching some kind of road. Look at the tire grooves."

Remembering how well Gene could observe things—from animal scat, to the flow of a river, to how to read water and spot the deadly rocks hidden underneath—I let him take the lead.

Noticing the tire marks on the ground, I observed, "Yeah, and there are more tire tracks over there. Why would there be so much traffic up here?"

"Well, let's see where the tracks lead. I'm sure they go somewhere."

"I hope they go somewhere soon cuz I really need to rest—and don't forget our picnic by the lake you promised me," I reminded him, as if my wishing would make it so.

Sam Spontaneity. It's a miracle we ever get from Point A to Point B the way he shuffles through life. Few concrete plans, just a wait-and-see attitude: "Let's see what develops."

Oh, how I've learned to savor the journey in two decades with that man! Thirty years in recovery have taught him to slow down and enjoy the ride more. We balance each other out; Gene is good for me.

"Gene, look at all the frigging dung on the road. What the hell is this?" I asked, sidestepping it wherever I could.

"Just follow the cow shit, babe. They're probably looking for water."

Of course! Farmers are herding the cows to the lake to drink. In one of the driest states in the Union, a lake is a gift anywhere. And just as I was thinking that, I saw a cow make a hasty exit into the woods.

"Did you see the cow? You're right! How much further, do you think?"

"Let's just keep walking."

Suddenly, it seemed like Christmas morning, a wondrous surprise. We had been hiking up that trail for three hours in search of a phantom lake. And then the ghost materialized: a gorgeous, unspoiled lake, a reservoir of water for wildlife living in the area. A respite for me and Gene to enjoy our packed lunch and remind ourselves why we often make the effort with our legs: to savor the beauty still left in the world and be grateful that, whatever happens to this endangered planet, we saw it before it disappeared into a memory.

Coming down the mountain was easier than going up. We

hated to leave such a hidden nugget in the middle of nowhere. But the orchard we took a break from was waiting for us. Shiro plums ready to fall off the tree, plucked instead by us to sell at the market, would be a real treat since they weren't for sale in stores.

Sunday would be a good day to offer our fruit for sale.

My life in recovery is like the surprise Indian paintbrush sprouting from the brown desert floor where I tried to grow a clump of purple flowers.

That stunning red flower.

WALKING
WITH EMILY

My doctor told me to walk a mile a day for the rest of my life to help the poor circulation in my legs. Keeping a sound body goes hand in hand with my spiritual recovery.

It's an easy mile up and down the island where I live in Puget Sound. Water is close by, the salt air blowing across Saratoga Passage when there's a west wind, colorful wildflowers—vivid pinks, yellows, blues, and purples—dotting both sides of the narrow road.

One morning, walking with my six-year-old granddaughter, Emily, I couldn't resist and picked a few of the prettiest ones to press between waxed paper at home. But she shamed me into putting them back, as if that would revive them. Flowers grow from their roots and lose their life source when cut.

People, Emily seemed to be reminding me, often have the power to recover from their wounds and regenerate themselves.

Even grow stronger.

THE SOUND
OF WATER

S ometimes, if we're lucky, we find ways to hold on to people and places in order to stay connected with them. Like
my brother, Gene grew up on a sailboat every summer. Sailing
is something we look forward to doing together on Puget Sound.
When Bill took me sailing, he taught me much of what I know
about the sport. I know what "close-hauled" and "running free"
mean. I relax when we "come about" because the wind is more
safely crossing the bow of the boat; then I tense up when I hear
"Jibe-ho!" careful not to get bumped into the water by a swinging
boom powered by a trailing wind.

Bill and I rarely see each other anymore, though we're in contact and try to keep each other in the loop. Both he and my sister
grieve deeply for their niece alongside me.

As I've grown in my recovery, I see my life through a different
lens. My childhood is clearer to me now. And I understand.

I still see my handsome brother at the tiller, an invisible presence sternly reminding me to trim the sails.

TAKING IT IN

O n my way to my friend's, my cell rang and I answered it. "Hi, Teri, I'm on my way." I was late once again. I'm usually pretty punctual, but I'd gotten on to New Mexico time after living there for nearly a decade.

"Where are you?" she asked. "I'm getting hungry." *Oh dear, she's mad.*

"I'm at Unser and Southern. I'll be there in ten minutes." Luckily, a state trooper hadn't seen me talking on the phone.

Six months had passed since I'd seen her, and she hadn't been well. I'd hoped to cheer her up.

Opening her front door, I crossed the threshold and gave her a lengthy hug.

"Oh, you look wonderful!" I said. "What did you do to your hair? I love it!"

Before she could answer me, five of my friends popped out from where they'd been hiding in the kitchen.

"Surprise! Happy Birthday!"

They all had their iPhones out, their cameras flashing. "Don't forget mine," I shouted. "I want this memory too!"

After they put their cameras down, we all composed ourselves.

Coming out of shock, I stammered, "But I'm January. You're three months late!"

"Ha! Just cuz you're on Camano Island most of the year doesn't mean we can't celebrate you!"

Celebrate me.

I had to turn seventy before I could do that with ease. I'd made big strides along the way: in my marriage, in my career, even with my children. I was thrilled they still wanted me around.

But all along that road while I was making progress, I had my crutches. Sometimes I still ate when I wasn't hungry and used alcohol for escape from the fears and disappointments in my life. This adult child only started to walk on her own when she gave up both three years ago.

Sitting around the table eating quiche with my friends, I felt teary, but they wanted a speech.

"This is a happy moment, ladies. The older I get, the more everything means to me. It's important to celebrate the things that bring me joy. I take nothing for granted anymore because I have more yesterdays than tomorrows. My life has been so blessed. Thank you for your friendship and celebrating with me today."

After cupcakes and coffee, I took one of my friends aside and shared some thoughts with her. Most of my friends at the celebration go to recovery meetings, and for them, as well as myself, it has become a way of life. This particular woman I had admired for several years.

"You know, Paula, I'm glad to have been in recovery this long. I don't think you would have liked me thirty years ago. It was difficult to relate to people. I didn't have many friends. And my kids, oh gosh, I was so self-absorbed, I wasn't there for them enough when they were growing up. But now two of them want me in their lives! I'm so lucky to get a second chance. That's why I bought the place on Camano—to be a part of my grandchildren's lives. You are all missed, of course, but how many people get do-overs like that?"

"Sure, I understand. You've been sorely tested."

Acknowledging her reference to Annie, I added, "Yes, well, that sadness lies in the back drawer, and I close it. Then opening the front drawers every day, I do the best I can with what I've got. Life goes on."

As I left the party, Teri waved goodbye and shouted, "Friendship isn't about miles!"

Well, that's a relief, I realized as I was driving away. *Otherwise I wouldn't have any!*

GRACE

While working at Harvard back in 1972, I spent a lot of time at a particular thrift shop in Cambridge. Making only about six thousand dollars a year, I was grateful to have acquired a taste for secondhand merchandise.

For twenty dollars, I bought a large print of Maxfield Parrish's most famous painting, *Daybreak*, mounted in a handsome frame. Something stirred in me as I spotted the alluring blues in an obscure corner of the shop where someone had placed the painting. It has held a prominent place over every bed I've slept in since that year.

I am the woman lying on the floor of the temple, one arm casually framing her face, shielding it from the sun. Columns support the temple, and there are leaves, water, rocks, and mountains in the background, painted in tranquil shades of blue.

Bending over me is a young undressed girl. I am in conversation with her. My face feels warm and I'm smiling. The setting in this picture is one of absolute calm, beauty, and serenity.

That has been my ever-present wish: to be as watched over and cared for, as it appears that woman was.

All my life, though I wasn't always awake and aware of it, I have been.

GOING BACK

Look back without staring.[23]

Three years ago I kept my promise to Eleni and went back to Greece for the third time. Gene anxiously awaited his visit to Santorini, one of Greece's volcanic islands in the Mediterranean and a geologic wonder. We landed in Athens at the end of September.

My friend had read in letters about the love of my life for more than two decades, and I daresay her mouth was watering; she was just dying to meet him. Eleni's memories of me, still buxom and lineless in early middle age, didn't match the reality when we saw each other. And her fantasies of Gene from many years before were better than the man who stood in front of her. Gravity does the worst damage to women, but it affects men as well, lining the pockets of plastic surgeons all over the world.

Eleni herself, her face deeply lined from years of sun damage and smoking, is a beautiful example of European women and their unapologetic attitude about age. *Good for you, Eleni, you can celebrate all that you are without the artifice of makeup or plastic surgery. I wish I had your self-confidence!*

Nineteen years is a long time. But feeling the warmth of her embrace and seeing her affirmation as our eyes locked onto each other, I felt as if no time had passed.

302

Together we stood in front of my old house in Politia, where I'd lived with my family thirty years before. And together we cried, the memories suddenly flooding and overwhelming us.

That house at 17 Pallados is dwarfed now by tall cypress trees along the sides. I had to peer through them at the whitewashed stucco balcony where my girls used to play and remembered Annie practicing gymnastics there with her best friend. The two-car driveway was still enclosed by locked gates, the first-story windows still barred.

The number 17 was hidden behind the overhanging branch of an orange tree, and buildings surrounded and overshadowed the house.

That evening after Gene had gone to bed, Eleni and I strolled into the plaza for a treat and sat down in an outdoor café.

"Two ice creams," my friend ordered. Then she turned to me. *"Ti thelis, mana mou?"*

"Vanilla, thanks," I said, then added, "with chocolate syrup."

"I'll have strawberry," she told the server as he scribbled our orders, "but mine with whipped cream."

I had waited to tell her in person about Annie, and when I did, my eyes tearing up, she shed no tears but said matter-of-factly as though she'd been in the recovery rooms for years, "Marilea, you cannot help her if she doesn't want help. Let her go. Concentrate on your other children and grandchildren."

"Yes, you're right, Eleni. I've spent fifteen years learning what you just told me in one minute."

"Bravo, Marilea," she concluded, taking my hand.

And timing is everything in life.

It wasn't until that moment that I could accept what she told me—without resistance.

We never spoke of Annie again.

The next day before we drove up to her beach house in Volos, I lit a candle for my daughter in the Greek Orthodox church nearby and prayed that she'd find peace—in this life or the next.

And I let her go.

During those three weeks that Gene and I spent in Greece— that redemptive journey—it all came back to me in waves: the pounding surf of grief in my heart, not just for Annie but for all the ignorance that had held me down and kept me from the light.

But I'm still here. I can laugh till my belly aches.

I've stopped chasing the butterfly.

THE GOOD GUEST

One of my all-time favorite movies is *Ben-Hur,* an old (1959) Charlton Heston movie about the crucifixion of Jesus Christ and the beginning of Christianity.

There's a scene where Judah has just enjoyed dinner with the sheik in his tent in the desert. Coming out of the tent, Sheik Ilderim looks at Judah expectantly. Judah returns the look, bewildered.

"Was the food not to your liking?" the sheik asks, a little miffed.

"Indeed!" Judah reassures him.

But the sheik needs more than Judah's word. He gently pounds his chest, signaling that his guest should burp to show his approval for dinner.

Judah obliges, and the near insult is forgotten.

In Greece, my friends also expected me to show my gratitude. Not by burping—by eating a lot. Either I could worry about my weight and watch every calorie that went into my mouth, or I could relax and be a good guest.

Eleni didn't know what obsessing over one's weight was all about, nor did she care.

I'm happy to have reached a point in my life where I didn't either.

Eleni and Nondas drove us high into the mountains of Makrinitsa on the Pelion Peninsula two or three times for lunch.

We watched the hunters with their long rifles going after wild boars. Eleni and I grabbed some bags and collected fallen chestnuts to roast back home. Their mellow flavor is surprisingly sweet, not what I would call "nutty flavored." That evening Eleni would chop them up, add some honey, and put the sauce on ice cream for dessert.

Lunch in the middle of the afternoon in exotic taverns involved no less than ten courses over two or three hours.

I would have been happy with the fava beans and the Greek salad with a week's worth of feta cheese on top, but that was just for starters. Next came a large platter of sausages, followed by squid. That squid must have cost a fortune just getting it up the mountain from Volos. But my friends spared no expense.

Then came a few more small courses, followed by "the omelette." Oh dear, that omelette dripping with oil had French fries, not the skinny, hard ones but the soft, fat ones, folded into it. I had no appetite by then, but I ate it. Delicious.

And then, of course, there was dessert. Enough *galaktoboureko*, a delectably rich custard, for a family of five.

For Gene and me.

While we were shoveling away about two hundred dollars' worth of food, our hosts were carefully watching us, more and more gratified with every bite that went into our mouths. That is how one is a good guest in Greece. And don't offer to go dutch. That's really insulting.

Our friends did encourage us to have some ouzo with lunch so we could take a nap. But Gene and I didn't go that far to be polite. We firmly refused the offer and drank water.

We managed those gargantuan lunches by going to bed early

and avoiding dinner. Breakfast for Greeks is often a ham sand-
wich around 11:00 a.m., but Eleni let me get away with coffee and
fruit. She knew I'd be starving by three o'clock.

There is no cure for addiction—whether it's alcohol, food, or
heroin—but I have learned to manage my eating disorder since
we all need to eat.

Like the other addictions, she's still an old friend who has out-
lived her usefulness in my life and sulks in a corner, wondering
why I don't want to play anymore.

COMING HOME

Stretched in his last-found home,
and knew the old no more.

—Oliver Wendell Holmes Sr.[24]

The chambered nautilus continuously grows new, larger cells into which it moves its internal organs.

Near the end of her life, my mother asked me to drive her to the beach, as if sitting in a new chamber of our lives, we'd breathe in the salt air together.

When I die, my bones will know the old no more; my children will sprinkle what's left of me over the ocean I love. There is no place on earth that feels more like home to me, the smell of its salt water uplifting me so.

SETTLEMENT DAY

O ur house on Camano Island came with a statue of the Virgin Mary in a small meditation garden in full view as you drive up the driveway. There's a delicate Japanese maple to her right and a bench to sit on.

When my son came to see the house, he took a picture of her. "Mom, maybe you could decorate her for Halloween!"

They all thought it was hilarious, but it annoyed me that I'd neglected to ask the sellers to haul her off when they left. I have had no luck getting anyone, from my gardener to the local priest, to take her away and put her in some other garden. And there are plenty of people up here who would appreciate having it.

But the statue must weigh half a ton. No one can carry it away.

Lately, though, I've been thinking that there's a reason why she's here—why she came with this, my hopefully last dwelling place in the whole world.

My childhood friend Juliette and I walked past another statue of the Virgin Mary on our way to school sixty-two years ago. And she suggested I might go to hell without the enlightenment of her religious faith. For a number of years I believed her.

Our individual lives took some interesting turns, and, in the end, I did find my way to living with an abundance of faith, if not Catholicism. And I would tell her, if I could, that hell was not arriving at the road to recovery sooner.

We used to watch network shows and movies at my house. I loved *The Lone Ranger*, *I Love Lucy*, and my favorite, *Father Knows Best*.

Julie, wherever you are, do you remember watching The Wizard of Oz? *Remember how when the movie concludes, Dorothy realizes that running away from Kansas was never the answer to her problems?* I, too, have discovered—after years of traveling around the world wondering if the change of scenery would make any difference—that I have always held the keys to self-fulfillment.

Dorothy had her three friends: the Scarecrow, who told her to use her brain and to open her eyes and recognize her good fortune; the Tin Man, who showed her how to look into her heart and appreciate and accept the love given to her; and the Cowardly Lion, who demonstrated the courage it takes to face life's difficulties without running away from them. My angels were my teachers.

Whatever "home" represents to Dorothy—of being a valued part of a family, of enjoying a communal feeling of love and acceptance, even a sense of completeness—it is her wish to go back there.

Glinda glided down from the sky in her pale pink dress with puffy sleeves, telling Dorothy she's always had the power to get home. All she has to do is click her heels together and repeat, "There's no place like home" three times. She and her dog, Toto, would be transported back to the farm in Kansas—to Auntie Em, Uncle Henry, and all the familiar faces she knows and loves. She'd be happy to be back there, no longer wishing she were somewhere else.

Where the yearning to be somewhere else vanishes . . .

Of course, Dorothy had those magically magnificent ruby slippers on.

But what do you expect?

That's Hollywood.

And did you get what

you wanted from this life, even so?
I did.
And what did you want?
To call myself beloved, to feel myself
beloved on this earth.

—Raymond Carver[25]

ENDNOTES

1. Rashani Réa, "The Unbroken," stanza 4, *Beyond Brokenness* (Bloomington: Xlibris, 2009), 171.
2. Bernard Malamud, *The Natural* (New York: Farrar, Straus and Giroux, 2003), 152. First published 1952 by Harcourt.
3. Theodor Seuss Geisel (Dr. Seuss), *Oh, the Places You'll Go!* (New York: Random House, 1990).
4. E. B. White, *Charlotte's Web* (New York: HarperCollins, 2012), 27. First published 1952 by Harper & Brothers.
5. Christina Baldwin, quoted in Janice Sterling Gaunt, *The Shame Game: Leaving Shame to Live in Abundance* (Dallas: Brown Books Publishing Group, 2011), Conclusion: "Words of Wisdom." Kindle.
6. Dory Previn, quoted in Karen Casey, *Each Day a New Beginning* (Center City: Hazelden Foundation, 1982), February 2.
7. Sue Monk Kidd, *The Secret Life of Bees* (New York: Penguin Books, 2003), 258. Kindle.
8. William Shakespeare, *The Tempest* (New York: Simon and Schuster, 1961), 13.
9. Theodor Seuss Geisel (Dr. Seuss), *Oh, the Places You'll Go!* (New York: Random House, 1990).
10. Laura Z. Hobson, *Gentleman's Agreement* (New York: Open Road Media, 2011), Chapter Six: "location 1297 and 1308." Kindle.
11. Sarah Darer Littman, *Purge* (New York: Scholastic Press, 2009), 154. Kindle.
12. "US Attaché Killed in Athens: Bomb in Parked Car Set Off as Officer Leaves His Home on Way to Embassy," *Los Angeles Times*, June 28, 1988.
13. Robin Worthington, quoted in Karen Casey, *Each Day a New Beginning* (Center City: Hazelden Foundation, 1982), May 8.

14. Theodor Seuss Geisel (Dr. Seuss), *Oh, the Places You'll Go!* (New York: Random House, 1990).
15. Emily Dickinson, "I'm Nobody! Who Are You?" Ralph W. Franklin (ed.), *The Poems of Emily Dickinson* (Cambridge, MA: The Belknap Press of Harvard University Press, 1998).
16. Deborah Meier, *The Power of Their Ideas* (Boston: Beacon Press, 2002), xi.
17. Virginia M. Axline, *Dibs: In Search of Self* (New York: Random House, 1964), 91. Kindle.
18. George Carlin, https://www.brainyquote.com/quotes/george_carlin_385217.
19. Recovery Family Groups, *Hope for Today* (Virginia Beach: Recovery Family Group Headquarters, Inc., 2002), 367.
20. Recovery Family Groups, *Hope for Today* (Virginia Beach: Recovery Family Group Headquarters, Inc., 2002), 173.
21. Judy Collins, quoted in Karen Casey, *Each Day a New Beginning* (Center City: Hazelden Foundation, 1982), January 24.
22. Elizabeth Goudge, quoted in Karen Casey, *Each Day a New Beginning* (Center City: Hazelden Foundation, 1982), April 4.
23. Recovery Family Groups, *Courage to Change* (New York: Recovery Family Group Headquarters, Inc., 1992), 216.
24. Oliver Wendell Holmes Sr., "The Chambered Nautilus," Leslie M. Pockell (ed.), *One Hundred Essential American Poems* (New York: St. Martin's Griffin, 2009), 62.
25. Raymond Carver, "Late Fragment," *A New Path to the Waterfall* (New York: Atlantic Monthly Press, 1990), 122. Copyright © 1989 by the Estate of Raymond Carver. Used by permission of Grove/Atlantic, Inc. Any third party use of this material, outside of this publication, is prohibited.

ACKNOWLEDGMENTS

With deepest gratitude, I bow to all of my angels. Their presence has spurred me on and given me the courage to be the best I can be. Friends and family have patiently watched and listened as I've journeyed through my life. They have taught me well.

My children and grandchildren: Carter, Annie, Caroline, Carrie, Catherine, and Emily

Gene, my loving partner of twenty-six years, and Angel, the father of my children

My recovery family: Allison and all of my sisters and brothers in Virginia, New Mexico, and Washington State

Mom, Dad, Bill, Lucy, Meg, Dodie, and Pris

Eleni, Juliette, and all of my friends

Irma Jackson, Madame Pelletier, and Doña Tini

My editors, Katie and Pamela, and all those at She Writes Press for their professionalism, caring, and support

Every one of my students

All of my animals

Special thanks to Rashani Réa, who wrote the poem "The Unbroken" in 1991, following the fifth death in her family. You can learn more about her at www.rashani.com.

ABOUT THE AUTHOR

Photo credit: Christopher Tuohy

Marilea grew up in a small Massachusetts town. Her marriage took her overseas, where she lived with her husband and children in the Foreign Service. After getting divorced, she taught English as a Second Language in Virginia for seventeen years.

She and her partner spend most of the year enjoying grandchildren, boats, and salt air on an island in Puget Sound. She also sings in a small women's choir. They still spend time in New Mexico, where they had lived after they retired.

Marilea received her master of arts (reflective practice) in teaching. In 2013 she joined Story Circle Network and began writing down and publishing her life stories. They have appeared in several publications, among them the SCN Anthologies and their journal. She has also contributed to *The Sober World* magazine. Much of her full-length work exposes a lifelong battle with substance use disorder, and the writing itself has proved to be cathartic and healing.

Marilea has a website, www.recoveryofthespirit.com, where she has blogged on the topic of addiction recovery since 2014. Her memoir, *Stepping Stones: A Memoir of Addiction, Loss, and Transformation*, is an inspiring tale of two journeys; her outward journey paralleled a sacred inner journey, where she sought a state of harmony and grace. Hers is a story of family fragmentation and years of emotional illness that led to various forms of addiction and sent her spiraling at several points into madness.

This is the story of her courageous struggle to fit the pieces together and, in the end, find her own road to happiness.

SELECTED TITLES FROM SHE WRITES PRESS

She Writes Press is an independent publishing company
founded to serve women writers everywhere.
Visit us at www.shewritespress.com.

The Coconut Latitudes: Secrets, Storms, and Survival in the Caribbean by Rita Gardner. $16.95, 978-1-63152-901-6. A haunting, lyrical memoir about a dysfunctional family's experiences in a reality far from the envisioned Eden—and the terrible cost of keeping secrets.

The S Word by Paolina Milana. $16.95, 978-1-63152-927-6. An insider's account of growing up with a schizophrenic mother, and the disastrous toll the illness—and her Sicilian Catholic family's code of secrecy—takes upon her young life.

Secrets in Big Sky Country: A Memoir by Mandy Smith. $16.95, 978-1-63152-814-9. A bold and unvarnished memoir about the shattering consequences of familial sexual abuse—and the strength it takes to overcome them.

The First Signs of April: A Memoir by Mary-Elizabeth Briscoe. $16.95, 978-1631522987. Briscoe explores the destructive patterns of unresolved grief and the importance of connection for true healing to occur in this inspirational memoir, which weaves through time to explore grief reactions to two very different losses: suicide and cancer.

Being Ana: A Memoir of Anorexia Nervosa by Shani Raviv. $16.95, 978-1631521393. In this fast-paced coming-of-age story, Raviv, spirals into anorexia as a misfit fourteen-year-old and spends the next ten years being "Ana" (as many anorexics call it)—until she finally faces the rude awakening that if she doesn't slow down, break her denial, and seek help, she will starve to death.

The Sportscaster's Daughter: A Memoir by Cindi Michael. $16.95, 978-1-63152-107-2. Despite being disowned by her father—sportscaster George Michael, said to be the man who inspired ESPN's *SportsCenter*—Cindi Michael manages financially and heals emotionally, ultimately finding confidence from within.